The *Quality* of Life

Books by Janet Lembke

Soup's On!: Sixty Hearty Soups
   You Can Stand Your Spoon In

Touching Earth: Reflections on the
   Restorative Power of Gardening

Tuscan Trees

Despicable Species

Shake Them 'Simmons Down

Skinny Dipping

Dangerous Birds

River Time

Janet Lembke

The *Quality* of Life

Living Well, Dying Well

The Lyons Press
Guilford, Connecticut
An imprint of The Globe Pequot Press

The Lyons Press is an imprint of The Globe Pequot Press.

10 9 8 7 6 5 4 3 2 1

Printed in the United States of America.

Book design and composition by Diane Gleba Hall.

Library of Congress Cataloging-in-Publication Data

Lembke, Janet.
    The quality of life : living well, dying well / Janet Lembke.
      p. cm.
Includes bibliographical references and index.
    ISBN 1-59228-128-1 (Hardcover)
    1. Terminally ill--Care. 2. Terminal care. 3. Terminally ill--Care.
4. Hospice care. I. Title.
R726.8.L455 2003
362.17'5--dc22
                                    2003021932

In memory of Sarah and the Chief,

both of whom lived life to the fullest

Contents

Acknowledgments

THIS BOOK did not spring into full being just from my own ideas and experience. Its sources are manifold and marvelous.

✦ Thanks are due first of all to the many good people—some named in the text, some pseudonymous—who shared their lives with me and told me their stories.

✦ And thanks to Polly Bart and Kerry Alexander, M.D., who contributed insights.

✦ Thanks also to James Nutt, who sent me pertinent Supreme Court cases.

✦ Thanks, too, to my writing group, the Good Old Girls (yes, some of us are definitely kin to rednecks), who listened to portions of this book and gave instructive comments: Judy Ayyildiz, Renée Crackel, Katie Lyle, Ann McCaig, Mary McKnight, Charlotte Morgan, Patty Pullen, Jeri Watts, and Toni Williams.

✦ Last, but not least, thanks to my truly supportive editor, Lilly Golden.

My gratitude to all of you is heartfelt.

The Companions

Living close to death
is not just a case of breath after breath.
It is to realize that to fraternize
with the dark prince is possible and wise,
so that in the final weather
when together you quit the room
though tentative and weary
you will have the enormous answer
to the enormous query.

—Josephine Jacobsen

In the Beginning

O may I join the choir invisible
Of those immortal dead who live again
In minds made better by their presence: live
In pulses stirred to generosity,
In deeds of daring rectitude, in scorn
For miserable aims that end with self,
In thoughts sublime that pierce the night like stars,
And with their mild persistence urge man's search
To vaster issues. . . .

—George Eliot, from "O may
I join the choir invisible"

I WOULD HAVE helped her die. I would have hugged her, given her the pills, along with a stiff Bloody Mary, and held her hand as she slipped from this world into the choir invisible. That's what my mother, when she was seventy-eight, still vigorous and competent, had said—no, insisted—that she wanted. And she received my glad promise to help ease her out when the time came. But when the kind of life she had wanted to escape descended upon her like a relentlessly deepening twilight, she had lost her ability to speak sensibly and was no longer capable of making rational decisions, nor had she been able to accomplish either of these acts since shortly after her second stroke. For four and a half years, then, I watched as she slid downhill, increasingly out of control of her basic bodily functions. She couldn't move spoon or cup to lips. A Foley catheter accompanied her everywhere; the plastic bag that filled remorselessly with dark yellow urine dangled from her bed, wheelchair, or recliner. Her bowels were cleaned out every three days by a licensed practical nurse. And for four and a half years, her heart kept pumping and her lungs, filling with air; she opened her mouth for food like a baby bird. Brute flesh, obeying primeval and mindless instinct, refused to let go. She was alive, yes, but hardly living. I could not, however, fulfill my promise, for she could neither sanction nor comprehend present and future events. The one grace granted her was that dementia made it impossible for her to understand her condition; at times she seemed almost happy. Just as often, though, she'd weep. How does one deal with someone who can no longer communicate nor reason? What is the best, most humane course? For all of those years, the best I could do was to watch the rise and fall of her chest as she breathed and to mourn her while she still lived. But in the end, I found a partial way to keep my promise.

To watch someone dying slowly, slowly over a span of years leads inevitably to a contemplation of the meaning of life. It has led me as well to consider some of the issues and phenomena surrounding death these days. Almost all of them seem to ignite both passionate support and furious opposition: living wills and powers of attorney, Elisabeth Kübler-Ross's explorations of the stages of dying, the current emphasis on a so-called "good death," right-to-die legislation, the hospice movement, and Oregon's legalization of assisted suicide for the terminally ill. And what about pulling the plug on people attached to life support? In 1976, that issue began to receive wide public debate with regard to Karen Ann Quinlan and has recently evinced itself in attempts by both Virginia and North Carolina to prevent legal guardians from removing life support from people who could not survive without it. The thinking was that removal would constitute neglect, if not outright murder. To let a grievously incapacitated person live or die—my elder daughter and I know that dilemma by heart, for we were forced in 1995, as the year slipped toward autumn, to decide yes or no on maintaining life support for my younger daughter. These matters are controversial enough, but add to them such entities as Dr. Jack Kevorkian and Derek Humphry's Hemlock Society, then the mixture becomes downright explosive.

These ways of trying to cope with our certain mortality are, every one of them, apparitions of confusion. How do we deal with life's end? How might we best approach it? Is quality of life a meaningful concept, or is it a purely subjective construct? Does human life hold an intrinsic sacredness?

I watched my once proud mother's witless and inexorable decline, pondered these questions, and found many others, including one that is hardly addressed at all in literature and popular thought: How best may those of us who have our wits about us care for old, frail people whose minds are lost forever in the shadows?

This is the story of my quest for answers to the hard but absorbing questions posed by our mortality, a condition that is as sure and immutable as the wheeling of the planet around the sun.

A Different Person

You can

                listen

                        for hours and

not hear it:

the ragged

                       body

spitting and whirring in

                    half-time.

              —Jeffery Beam, "The Stroke"

WHO WAS SHE before two massive strokes turned her into someone else? The name her mother gave her was Sarah. She was born at home in Staunton, Virginia, one of the Shenandoah Valley's farm-to-market towns; the year was 1911. Her voice, to the last of her ability to speak, was graced with a soft southern accent, not the plummy richness of the Carolinas nor the language of the Virginia piedmont influenced long ago by British colonists, but rather a gentling of hard consonants and a tendency to linger fondly over words. And she was blessed with more energy than a whole passel of puppies. Hyperkinesis is the fancy way of putting it. But in her it was benign, not destructive. In her adult life before the strokes, she used it for rearing five children, for entertaining and travel, for church and community, and, always, for voluntarism on a scale so generous, so lavish that it would wear most people out before they'd half-started.

During World War II, while my father served in the Army in both the United States and England, my mother brought me and my two younger brothers, Joe and Bob, to Staunton to live with her mother. When the war ended, we made our way back north. But my father, in love with the Valley and its green pastures, bought a farm near Staunton. He and my mother, Joe, Bob, and my two post-war sisters, Sarah Jane and Ginny, moved south to the state for which Ginny had been named. A brand-new college graduate, I stayed in the north, soon married, and bore children. We visited often, but the contact was fleeting and focused on fun, food, and expeditions, like driving over the Blue Ridge to see Thomas Jefferson's home, Monticello, or exploring one of the many caverns that riddle the Appalachians like holes in a great limestone cheese. But beginning in the late '70s, I came to know her as a woman as well as a mother. It was then, with only one of my four children still at home, that I took advantage of my newly single state and moved back to the town of my childhood and early adolescence. My apartment, located in the spacious basement of an 1840s house built on a steep hill, was eight doors away from her house. Eight doors away, that is, from her excellent dinner parties and her indispensable laundry equipment.

Not unnaturally, we started talking about everything from recipes to politics and religion. A devout woman, then in her late sixties, she was serving as an elder in her church, but she relished startling her compeers in the congregation. "There are four things wrong with Jesus," she'd say to the members of her adult Sunday-school class. "He never married, he never had children, he didn't grow old, and he wasn't a woman." She delighted in recounting her listeners' perturbation. Her talk was not malicious, however, but rather designed to trigger thought in people unaccustomed to examining, much less questioning, traditional beliefs.

In 1987, when she was seventy-six years old, I decided to record her stories on tape, from her childhood in a small Southern place to her courtship and marriage, and on to child-rearing, her wartime experiences, and whatever else presented itself. It was necessary, however, to make appointments to see her and capture her tales. For as long as I could remember, her days were filled from dawn till well after dark with an omnium-gatherum of activities, most of them centered on community service. She started volunteering before World War II and kept at it unabated till illness incapacitated her. The list of organizations for which she worked, often at the highest levels, is long: president of the Junior League of Cleveland, two-term member of the Board of Visitors for the Virginia School for the Deaf and Blind, regent of a chapter of the D.A.R., early member of the local branch of Literacy Volunteers of America, and founder of a mediation center serving Staunton and the surrounding area. The only paying job that she held was one to which she was elected—city councilwoman.

Such bustle, such devotion! It took me years to see it, but in one sense, all of those commitments and a legion of others, some sequential, some simultaneous, amounted to running away from home. Her husband, my father, was, from early in the marriage until his death in 1972, a bingeing alcoholic, sometimes calm and smiling, sometimes loud and completely loco. The rest of the family did not know from day to day whether we'd be living with Dr. Jekyll, who was informative and entertaining, or Mr. Hyde, who was one-hundred-and-eighty degrees the other way. He was also possessed of enough money to stay at home and not go off to work at all, though he did fancy politics and served several terms in the Ohio State Senate. Voluntarism was my mother's escape. It got her out of the house and into a world that did not fly into unpredictable rages and then pass out. As it happened, she had a genius for service. Her work with Literacy Volunteers was recognized when President George Bush the elder named her in 1990 as number 170 of his thousand Points of Light.

For five Octobers, I made an appointment with her so that we could talk about her life and times. She was becoming physically frail at that time, her height diminished eight inches by osteoporosis, which had also hunched her back, but her intellect, her verve crackled with energy. Tape recorder and notebook in hand, I'd arrive at the scheduled hour, and we'd go, along with Muffin, her white toy poodle, to her living room, which was filled with Victoriana—sofa, rocking chair, armchairs and side chairs with deeply carved walnut frames and turquoise upholstery. Seating ourselves on the sofa, we'd converse and look at a trove of photographs for a whole morning, while the grandmother clock in the corner delivered Westminster chimes on the quarter-hour and sonorous, talk-interrupting *bongs* on the hour. The clock, not so tall as a grandfather clock, had been built by a local craftsman of great skill, who also kept Thomas Jefferson's clock at Monticello in good working order. I also inveigled Sarah into a class on memoir writing that I led in 1987 as part of the evening extension program at the local college. That was the period in which our relationship ceased being that of just mother and daughter; instead, we talked more as two grown women who'd known each other for a long time. But she'd never been the kind of mother who tried, consciously or not, to regard her grown offspring as children. Commenting only yea or nay about our enterprises, she had always had the grace to say no more and let us soar or fall flat on our faces. The latter was far more instructive than any nagging disapproval could have been. When we succeeded, though, she'd pause to cheer before returning to her own activities. I found it easy to ask her questions. Some were lighthearted: What games did you play as a child? What were your favorite books? Others homed in on the facts of life: Tell about childbirth in your day. Still others looked at the darker aspects of her experience: How did you feel at the tender age of sixteen when your father died? And, how did you manage to live with my father's alcoholism? Later, I'd transcribe the taped material, edit it for continuity, and illustrate it with appropriate photographs—Sarah in her sandbox, Sarah in her wedding dress surrounded by bridesmaids, Sarah with grandchildren. Her life spanned gaslights and electricity, horsedrawn carriages and automobiles, nuclear innocence and nuclear knowledge, peace and war. She had entered the world of technology along with the century. Each year's segment of the story—I called it *The Book of Sarah*—was given at Christmas to my brothers and sisters and to Sarah herself.

She answered my questions in detail and also offered many stories that I didn't know enough to ask about. One remembered Hallowe'en trick-or-treating. She and her sister, elder by two years, would parade up and down Main Street escorted by their household's factotum, a stout black woman whom my mother called Mammy. The children were dressed up, of course, as witches or fairies. Mammy was dressed up, too, wearing the mortarboard and robes in which Sarah's father had graduated from law school at the University of Virginia.

Another story dealt with her weeks at summer camp, not a fancy camp such as children are sent to nowadays but rather a farm in the country, where several little girls from town could participate in rural activities—hiking, riding horses, swimming with water wings in a nearby river, harvesting and wolfing down summer-fresh food. After they'd gone to bed, they'd giggle-whisper about life and its peculiarities. "At that camp," my mother said, "I heard my first dirty joke. I didn't know about dirty jokes then. Just knew it was something you wouldn't talk about in public. And I certainly didn't understand it at the time. All those years ago, and I've never told it to anyone." Nor did she keep me in suspense: Once upon a time, a young man, recognizing an important gap in his store of knowledge, sought advice from an experienced friend about what to do on his wedding night. He was told to put the longest thing into the hairiest thing. And when the magical moment finally came, ah, he put his nose into her armpit. I had to turn off the tape recorder until we stopped laughing.

Much of our talk was far more sober. When I asked about her father, who had died at home in his own bed from tuberculosis when she was a senior in high school, Sarah said, "He was a quiet man. I really didn't know him." And she hadn't. He spent much of his time with work and friends; on weekends, he and his male cronies would often go to a cabin in the mountains, where, for all Sarah knew, they may have gone hunting or fishing, may have caroused, or both. Speculation has it that he was an alcoholic. She, her sister, and, later, her brother slept with their mother in her bedroom. "But," she said, "our mother must have gone to visit him every so often."

I also heard the tale of Sarah's journey west with my father after their marriage in September, 1929, a month before the stock market crashed and the Depression came lumbering in to squat on the economy like a dark, broody bird until the early days of World War II. She was eighteen, and he, twenty. Both had been enrolled in Eastern colleges, Wellesley and Yale, neither of which in that day permitted married students to attend. Few schools did. But Stanford University in Palo Alto, California, was among the few. So off the couple went, rolling west in a shiny black Model A Ford and taking pictures along the way. Oh, he was handsome then, and she, dark-haired, tall, and lithe, in a coat with a fur collar and a cloche hat. Snapshots show her standing below the rock wall of El Capitan in Yosemite National Park and sitting on the steps of the small, vine-covered Palo Alto cottage in which she and my father lived when they attended Stanford. There, she became pregnant for the first time. Late in the pregnancy, the child was stillborn. She never learned whether it was a boy or a girl.

As for her husband, he was a good-timing man from the word "go." His alcoholism became apparent within the decade after the wedding. And how did Sarah view it? For the next thirty years, she chose mostly not to see it or to find silver linings in its huge dark cloud—that her husband was a good man, devoted to his children and his home. In September, 1972, in the last week of his life, when it was clear to her that he was dying, she kept him at home on the sofa-bed in the TV room that had once, in the last half of the 1800s, served as the main house's detached kitchen. In 1972, we children were all grown and living away from home. Nor did she tell any of us that he was dying, an omission that I resented until I realized, several years later, that if we knew nothing, then we could do nothing. We could not interfere with her decision to keep him at home. Had she told us, we would, I am certain, have gone into full gear to put him into the hospital. That was not what she wished. She had the grace to let him go when his time came. She told me that his death was peaceful and without pain. I know now with my whole heart that she was right.

The one thing that I did not ask Sarah—that I regret not asking her—was about the death of her mother, Jannette, the grandmother for whom I am named. I can piece together some of that story, and I have a poem that Jannette penciled inside the back cover of *The Runner's Bible,* a book published in 1915 and treasured by my mother after my grandmother's death. Though Jannette does not acknowledge its author, the poem, written by William Allingham (1820-1889), clearly expresses her sentiments on death. I present it not in Allingham's stanzas but as she inscribed it.

When I am Gone

No funeral gloom, my dears,
    when I am gone
Corpse gazing—tears—
    black raiment
    graveyard grimness
Think of me as withdrawn
    into the dimness
Yours still, you mine
Remember all the best
    in past memories
    forget the rest
And so to where I wait
Come gently on.

"No dimness," my mother said. "After I die, I'll come back as a rainbow." And she surrounded herself with rainbows. A candle-holder with dangling prisms cast rainbows on her living room wall. A rainbow arched across her checks and on all twelve pages of a month-by-month calendar with gorgeous photographs. The calendar, saved after its year was up, was later used to decorate the walls of her bathroom: sit upon the commode, gaze upon a future incarnation.

When my parents moved south, they bought the house next door to the one in which my grandmother lived. Hers was a mid-1800s red-brick house with white columns on either side of the front door. It was the house from which my mother was married; the house in which Joe, Bob, and I spent the years of World War II. With our father away with the military and our mother off doing work for the Red Cross, our grandmother brought us up, teaching us manners, insisting that we bathe every day, and exercising full dictatorial powers in every other respect. I fumed then; I'm grateful now. In 1966, when Jannette reached the august age of ninety, it became clear that she'd arrived at the point of needing daily help, and much of it. Sarah lived at home during the day (or in some venue of her volunteering) but went next door to spend each night with her mother. During the daylit hours, Mary Cabell, a plump, infinitely cheerful, middle-aged black woman who had long been both Jannette's household help and her bosom companion, provided care. The two of them nursed her for three years, bathing her, feeding her, calming her fears. The objective was always to let Jannette live to the end in her own home, with the corollary that she not be subjected to the impersonal treatment that might be expected from hired strangers.

So, from Sarah's experience, by Sarah's example, her children could make a close guess about what she might want. It became more than a close guess during a journey that she and I made through the Midwest in the spring of 1989. Every year, my high school in Cleveland invites a member of the class that had graduated forty years ago to present a talk to the faculty and student body. I was thrilled to be asked. My mother, learning of the trip, said that if it suited, she'd like to come along to visit old friends on the banks of Lake Erie. Good idea, but before I'd even had the chance to agree, she'd begun to plan other visits that we might make as long as we were in the area—a nephew in Detroit, a niece in Evanston, Illinois, my elder daughter and her family in the northwestern corner of Wisconsin. We spent three weeks on the road, and we talked, oh, we talked.

At that time she was less than a month shy of her seventy-eighth birthday. By then age and osteoporosis had truly stolen her physical vigor. I suspect that she also had osteoarthritis in her knees and perhaps her hands. Her answer to pain, however, was not to consult a doctor; she was allergic to the very idea—forget about the actuality—of medical people, treatments, surgeries, pills. She said, "Remember that I'll be a rainbow," and she relied on willpower to help her overlook discomfort and a no-nonsense, heavy-duty aluminum cane to stabilize her walking and take some of the weight off her legs. On our expedition through the Midwest, Sarah wielded that cane like a rod, parting a crowd in the entrance to a restaurant like Moses parting the Red Sea. Nor did the multitudes ever seem to mind but smiled and nodded in greeting. She'd waltz to a table, while I followed happily in her wake. Her decrepitude was only physical, however; her mind and energy were still operating at full speed ahead.

The conversations began as soon as we launched ourselves toward Cleveland. And the first major topic broached was Sarah's wish to sell her house, an 1840s Federal-style dwelling of gray-painted brick, in which she'd reared my sisters, in which her husband had died, in which she'd tutored literacy clients and conducted planning sessions and tea-party fundraisers for all her enterprises. There, year after year, she had regularly provided Thanksgiving and Christmas feasts for at least thirty people, including students from countries such as Nigeria, Indonesia, Japan, mainland China, Taiwan, and Thailand, all so far away that it was not easy to go home during college breaks. The house was, as she often declared, a "woman-killer." Yes, it was—three stories, not counting the attic, with six bedrooms, four baths, manorial living room and dining room with nineteenth-century mantels and twelve-foot ceilings, library, telephone room, kitchen, break-fast room, and TV room, home to a huge fireplace, that had once been used for roasting meats and baking bread. An old house of that size entails much maintenance. It also features long, steep stairs. Because Sarah was experiencing physical difficulty with the daily chores and with getting from upstairs to downstairs and back again, she had decided that she wanted to move to a smaller abode with a bedroom and bath on the first floor. She talked the idea over with me for the whole three weeks of our expedition, and as soon as we reached home, before we'd so much as un-packed, she called a realtor. My brother Bob, well into his fifties, objected strenuously when he heard that she'd put the house on the market. Indignantly, he told her, "You're selling my *child-hood*." She offered it to him; she offered it to the other four of us. But each of us had a home, and none of us wanted to take on the care of a classically beautiful woman-killer, even though it figures on Virginia's register of historic houses. It sold lickety-split, and in almost no time at all, she'd rented a considerably smaller frame house, located just around the corner, with a bedroom and bath on the first floor.

It was on our Midwestern trip that Sarah talked about becom-ing a rainbow—that is, about her eventual death. Or, not so much about death and dying as her fear of losing vigor and having to endure pain. And she asked me if, when the time came, I'd help give her Godspeed out of this world. Yes. Not only could I help, but I also had access to the proper drugs through my elder daughter, who is a veterinarian. Before that moment came, however, my mother wished not to burden us, her children, with her increasing debility. She'd move into Sunnyside, a retirement community of sterling reputation that was sponsored by her church. It offered tripartite services: independent living, assisted living, and nursing care. Most residents moved in when they were still capable of fending for themselves, a few were accepted directly into the assisted living facility, but none were admitted who had gone past the assisted-living phase and needed all-out nursing. She was definite about her wish to end her days from Sunnyside, where many of her friends and colleagues had established residence. Not *at* it, but *from* it, for I'd come to get her for a home visit.

We were fantasizing. It was hardly a realistic plan.

In the fall of 1992, when she was eighty-one, a blood vessel burst in her brain: stroke. It was not caused by a disease, like high blood pressure, that is amenable to medication but rather by an untreatable condition called amyloid angiopathy, in which amyloid, an insoluble protein, is deposited in the walls of arteries supplying the brain. It thins the arteries and may break them, an event that leads to intracerebral hemorrhages. The stroke slowed her speech and made her grope for words, but she suffered no paralysis. In the rehabilitation center that she entered immediately on leaving the hospital, she talked frequently, urgently about going straight to Sunnyside after returning home. And Sunnyside was willing to accept her as an assisted-living resident. But once at home again, the plan to leave familiar surroundings receded and soon disappeared, for she rebounded well, regaining most of her old abilities, though, on a word from her doctor, the Department of Motor Vehicles sent her written notice that her driver's license had been suspended but would be restored if she could pass a test.

She obtained the manual of rules and regulations and may have studied it, but she never asked any of us to take her to the DMV for testing. Her partial aphasia remained stubborn. But if a simple word eluded her, she'd come up with a double-barreled doozy— "cogitate" instead of "think," "hornswoggle" for "deceive." Her greatest triumph was getting disconnected from the Foley catheter that she'd come home with from the hospital and rehab center: She learned both to hold her urine and to pee again at will. In the all-important realm of voluntarism, she certainly engaged herself heart and soul in the programs of the county mediation center that she had founded. She also went into the basement one morning the following spring, when my sister Ginny, her youngest daughter, had come from Texas to visit. There, in Ginny's presence, she extracted the Sunnyside papers from her tall filing cabinet and reduced them to confetti.

Was she convinced that she'd recover completely, that her time to become a rainbow was still in the distant future? Was she thumbing her nose and sticking out her tongue at death? Or was she somehow certain that we would care for her at home as she'd cared for her mother and, four years later, our father? Yet, she was clearly afraid, though she did not say so. Tearing up the papers was a classic act of denial.

But she had become a different person, timorous about being left alone. She wore a Lifeline pendant around her neck, a lightweight unit that could be worn with complete safety when she bathed. It is a round disk with a central button that she could press to summon help should she suffer an accident in her house or yard. She played tennis ball toss-and-fetch with her little poodle, Muffin. We hired Rosa and Grace, licensed practical nurses, to stay with her at night. No-nonsense Rosa, a one-time cateress, was hefty and black, while Grace, who'd long known

Sarah and named a daughter for her, was white and unrepen-
tantly bossy. Both were highly competent. When the man from
whom Sarah had rented the house returned to Staunton, Rosa
and Grace went with her to a nearby townhouse.

But Sarah was alone in the townhouse at dusk in the fall of
1993, dressing to go out for dinner, when the second stroke felled
her, only a year after the first. She retained wit enough to use the
Lifeline to summon help. But this time, the broken artery leaked
considerable blood into her brain, creating a swelling—a hematoma—that exerted enough pressure to give her what must have
been a most excruciating headache. Hair shaved, skull skillfully
breached, she underwent surgery to remove the hematoma the day
after entering the hospital. This time she did not go to the rehab
center on discharge a week after being hospitalized but, for
bureaucratic reasons, went into the skilled-care facility of a local
nursing home, which I'll call Blue Sky Manor (it figures later in the
story). She would stay there until she had regained some compe-
tence and, more important, until the rehab center had an opening.

Ah, the reach and not-so-occasional wrong-headedness of
Medicare! It covers both hospitalizations and in-patient rehabilitation programs. But in a high-handed rule that I find hard to comprehend—though it may speak to the possibility that some
people would not hesitate to hornswoggle the federal Medicare
program—it dictates that its insurance coverage for rehab ceases
the moment a patient goes home after leaving the hospital. And if
the patient should then go from home into a rehab center, coverage does not kick in again. Under this rule, the only acceptable
way to bridge the gap between hospital and rehab is not to go
home at all but rather to enter an impersonal place that offers
nursing care. The rule implies that skilled nursing cannot be done
at home, and it completely ignores the relative inexpensiveness

of treatment when the patient resides in familiar, friendly surroundings.

Rosa and Grace went with her to Blue Sky Manor to care for her during the day. One morning, not long after she'd arrived at the place—an ominous flesh-pink stucco building that usually had a kettle of turkey vultures soaring overhead—I went with my husband, a retired Navy man whom I call the Chief, to visit her. Wheelchair-bound, she was almost completely aphasic. But her mind was still working. We talked to her; she nodded in comprehension, though we could not make clear the reason for her nursing-home stay. Toward the end of our visit, she shook her head and frowned. Then she drew her right index finger across her throat. Grace, who was present, told us later, "Sarah is saying she'd like to cut me off." Though we did not disagree, we read the gesture in quite another way: She realized that she was in a place that even her worst fears had never conjured. She wanted out. She was reminding me of my promise.

But it was much too late for me to act. Her grasp on reason was no longer firm.

STROKE: I set out to learn about this shattering vascular event. It is the third leading cause of death, after heart disease and cancer; it is the prime cause of disability. Thirty percent of strokes occur in people under sixty-five, but the incidence of stroke doubles in each decade after the age of fifty-five. It strikes more women each year than men, but the figures for both exceed 100,000. 160,000 people die of it annually. And every year accounts for 750,000 new or recurrent strokes.

I would find the figures remote except that my mother illustrates them.

THREE WEEKS AFTER entering Blue Sky Manor, Sarah leaves it
for a month of therapy at the rehab center. Then, five weeks later,
in January, 1994, she finally comes home. Rosa remains on duty,
but Grace departs to tend to her own family. Thus, the first order
of the day is to search for a team of round-the-clock caregivers
who will act cooperatively rather than engage in backbiting and
shiftlessness. Noting the parade of probationary workers, Sarah
smiles and says in her new little-girl voice, "They come and go. I
say hello." Though the tone of voice is a post-stroke development,
the ability to construct a jingle at the slightest provocation must
date back to the time that she really was a little girl. By May, however, we do manage to put in place a pleasant, well-trained three-
some—a certified nurse's assistant, a young single mother with
much experience in elder care, and Rosa, in charge.

Death by Choice

So proud she was to die
    It made us all ashamed
That what we cherished, so unknown
    To her desire seemed.

So satisfied to go
    Where none of us should be,
Immediately, that anguish stooped
    Almost to jealousy.

                    —Emily Dickinson

COULD I REALLY have given my mother the Bloody Mary and the pills? Many people have helped a family member die. Some have left first-hand accounts. And I know several women who have assisted their mothers in leaving this world. Their stories, two sorrowful but calm, the other wrenching, will be told, along with some other accounts, after a quick look at the literary records.

One of the best known is that of Betty Rollin, television journalist and survivor of breast cancer, who wrote in *Last Wish* of her mother's desire to die. When Ida, ravaged by ovarian cancer, asked Betty for help, she assured her daughter that she'd had a good life and was ready to let it go. But, as Betty writes, "The problem was that death did not oblige," though Ida was suffering considerable pain. Betty and her husband then spent much time researching the methods and pitfalls of helping Ida to achieve her goal. Information on pills, the kind and the dosage to ease her out, was hard to come by, nor was it easy to find physicians willing to talk about the matter. On the other hand, the pitfalls were obvious from the beginning. Chief among them was the possibility that if there was any suspicion that Ida's suicide was assisted, Betty might be indicted for murder. A grand concatenation of both persistence on Ida's part and sheer chance led to the resolution that Ida desired. It was she who persuaded her doctor to prescribe the pills, she who rescheduled the home-care nurses, put off potential calls by well-meaning relatives, and so arranged to take the medicaments when she was assured of being alone. Betty records that not long before she took the pills, Ida said to her, "What do people do who don't have children? What if you want to get out and you have no one to help you?" *Last Wish* presents a brave and moving account of a mother and daughter conspiring together to realize the mother's deeply held wish. And it speaks eloquently to the current debate on suicide for people who are elderly and ill: to permit assistance or to prohibit it.

Another writer, Jessamyn West, known for her many novels that notably include *The Friendly Persuasion* and *Cress Delahanty*, has also written an account of giving end-of-life support to her younger sister, Carmen. The story, tender yet unsentimental, is told in her 1976 memoir *The Woman Said Yes*. Carmen, laid low by colon cancer, wrote an urgent summons: "Sister, dear sister, come home and help me die." And the narrator, into whose four-year-old arms Carmen had been placed just after she was born, responded without hesitation, feeling that it was far better to be with a dying sister than to be elsewhere. She writes: "All of us know that someday we will die. If there were a chance that we would not die, then we might be on the rack; might not be able to stop hoping and wondering and fearing. Carmen had been taken off the rack. There was no more hope for life. There was now an energetic and almost gay period of planning the kind of death she chose: the kind of death and at the time she chose. *She* had not chosen death: fate or genes, or God, which is perhaps the name we give that combination, had made the choice. She at least intended to have some voice in the matter."

Jessamyn West points out that once upon a not-far-distant time, Christian burial was denied to anyone who committed suicide. Instead, the body would be consigned to burial at a cross-roads, a stake through its heart. And she points out a persistent irony: An act intended to bring about death, even if the would-be suicide survives the attempt, is not a punishable crime, but the moment that another person takes on a role—giving an injection, a pill, or simply a shove into harm's way, that person has provided illegal assistance. The narrator and Carmen faced this dilemma and others. And the teller of the tale remembers the two months that she lived with her mortally ill sister: "We were planners, technicians, plotters, true. And the goal of our planning was death. But we had all the verve of generals planning a battle: death would occur, certainly; the battle could not be waged without that, but the battle plan itself should consider all possibilities of setbacks and miscarriages and reverses. The battle itself should not fail because of inadequate planning." How many pills were needed to end Carmen's life? By what suspicion-quelling means could they keep the housekeeper and the day nurse away on Carmen's final day? The presence of either of these people would have precipitated an unwished-for trip to the hospital, where the best that could be done would be to pump Carmen's stomach and prolong her nearly unbearable pain. Unlike Betty Rollin's mother, who thought that it was safer that no one else be with her when she died, Carmen wished for her sister's presence and had it firmly until the end.

Assistance is not just women's work. Yet another story is told by Sam Wright in his autobiographical book *Koviashuvik: Making a Home in the Brooks Range,* which was published in 1989. He and his wife, Billie, lived north of the Arctic Circle in a log cabin of their own building amid those glacier-covered peaks. Sam Wright, once a faculty member at the Graduate Theological Union in Berkeley, California, describes the time spent there as an "adventure of this sacred journey that we all share"—the journey of being alive. From that base, for twenty years, they gave their voices and energies in behalf of preserving Alaska's greatest resource, the wilderness. But in 1987 Billie fell ill with breast cancer, which entailed an operation and chemotherapy. No more than four months later, the quality of her life had become so diminished that she no longer wanted to keep living. She was in Arizona at the time, too ill to make the journey home to her beloved mountains. Sam Wright tells of the moment: "On December 7, a day she picked because it was Pearl Harbor Day and 'It might be the beginning of world peace as Gorbachev of the Soviet Union is visiting the President of the United States,' Billie delivered herself from the trauma and indignity of a lingering death and died in my arms." The following summer he scattered her ashes at her behest "on the knoll where the cranberries at Koviashuvik grow the thickest and finest."

In these accounts of suicide in response to intolerable illness, there is no sign of culpability in those who assist at the death of someone they love. There is no guilt. Instead, moral certainty shines clear: the decision to die was comforting and right to the person who made it; the death itself represents a triumph over illness and indignity, and the survivor who helped is not only consoled but strengthened by these beliefs. Nor is such assisted dying a phenomenon of modern times: Patrick Henry, who said, "Give me liberty or give me death" in another context, chose death as surcease from the pain caused by a severe intestinal blockage that his physician could not cure. An eyewitness has left an account of the occasion. The physician, Dr. Cabell, handed his patient a vial of calomel, or mercury chloride, whereupon, after a prayer, Henry drank it and died.

The impressions of consolation and rightness are given weight when I talk with a woman who asks me to call her Neal. She is possessed of eyes as blue as a mountain lake; her smile is ready and wide; her short, straight hair shows broad bands of white, which began to appear when she was only twenty-one. Now in her late fifties, she works as the business manager of a landscaping company, and while we talk, her own yard roars with the sounds of a John Deere lawn tractor mowing the grass amid islands of magnolias and maples. Luckily, the sounds come through faintly on the tape of our conversation.

It takes a little time for Neal to segue into her story, which cannot be easy to tell, especially to a stranger. When she reaches stride, she says, "I was raised to help my parents out when the time came. Of the three children, I was the only one both my parents spoke to of dying. They made it perfectly clear that they didn't want to lose any quality of life. I would say that both my parents died of terminal pride. I mean, they took their own lives, but it had to do with what they were willing to accept from others. From early childhood, they made it perfectly clear by telling me stories, like Eskimos going off on the ice. The idea of helping my parents die has been educated into me. The actual doing of it is another thing, but the idea has been there all my life."

She did not help her father, who had started to have minor strokes. As a physician, he had seen enough people kept messily alive beyond good reason to live. One day, early in the morning, he drove his car into a stone wall. Hindsight and Neal's mother's recollections of the days preceding the crash make it clear that the act was intentional.

Neal reminisces about her mother's life. Miz Jones on many occasions exhibited world-class eccentricity, probably as a result of damage from a brain hemorrhage and a subsequent operation when she was in her thirties. Shortly after the operation, she came to believe that she had never been baptized, at least not to her knowledge. When she decided that it was time to rectify this omission, she lived with her family in a small town in the deepest South, and after considerable thought, she chose the Episcopal Church. There she told the priest, "I've studied it, and I really think the Christian myth is a lovely story. And if it's all right with you—mind you, I cannot buy the virgin birth and a few other things—but if it's all right with you, I'd like to be baptized in the Episcopal Church." The priest said no, he wouldn't do it because she'd need to be able to say the Apostles' Creed, which states, in a modern translation, that Christ "was conceived by the power of the Holy Spirit and born of the Virgin Mary." On another occasion, she answered the door to find an evangelist standing there holding a Bible in such a fashion that the words "Holy Bible" faced her directly. She knew that he intended her to see them. And he spoke: "Does Jesus live here?" "Yes, he does," she said, turning to the front of the house and calling loudly, "*Jesus!*" Neal says that as a teenager she died a thousand deaths when her mother told this story. "She said that the boy lost all color, and then a lot of color came back. Then he just left. For years I thought somebody was going to stop me and tell me my mother was going straight to Hell."

Not even with safeguards was Miz Jones to be made dependably civil. Neal tells of a reception in which her parents comprised the receiving line. Her mother had been tutored beforehand: If her husband said, "I'd like to introduce you to so and so," then she was to respond, "How nice to meet you." If he said, "You remember so and so," she was to say, "Nice to see you again." The line, however, began to back up, and a woman tried to make small talk with Miz Jones. She said, "My, there are a lot of people here." And Miz Jones replied, "Yes, there are more people than chairs, and God knows I have enough chairs."

Neal comments on these moments by saying that as a teenager she saw her mother's behavior as horrifying, but as an adult, she finds it endearing.

In the mid-'90s, Neal was summoned home by her mother, then in her mid-seventies, a diabetic and cancer survivor as well as victim of mini-strokes and congestive heart failure. Doctors had recently performed tests and proposed surgery to clear out a carotid artery that was ninety percent blocked. Neal's younger brother, a doctor, who favored the operation, had started looking for a place in which their mother could recover and subsequently stay without being burdened by the chores of independent living. "But she was just bound and determined," Neal says, "that her freedom was not going to be turned over to doctors or nurses or nursing homes. You inherit a tendency toward euthanasia. Miz Jones's sister Jean, we are sure, had taken her life because it was time to go to a nursing home and give up her independence. And my brother, unknowingly, said to Mom, 'I'll be looking. Just plan on going to a nursing home.' But when Mother hung up the phone, she looked at me clear-eyed, and she said, 'I guess it's time to go find out what Aunt Jean is up to.'"

It is preemptive suicide that Neal's mother chose—an act done not to put an end to present pain but to prevent debilitation in the future, a sure event that she found horrifying to contemplate. Neal and her brother each offered to build an addition to their homes. "But that was not what she wanted. She didn't want ever to come to the point where we were cleaning up after her, that she wasn't in charge." They talked then about the wish to cease living. Her mother was fully determined to go ahead. When would it be? The day of the initial conversation was Monday. Her mother named Thursday.

Neal smiles broadly, remembering that final visit, in which she and her mother were, in Jessamyn West's words, "planners, plotters, technicians." "We had three full days of knowing when she wanted to do it. There were people she wanted to talk to. There were foods she wanted to eat. Because she was a diabetic, they were things normally forbidden to someone in her condition." Neal confesses then that she'd also like a forbidden treat if she knew she were headed rapidly, deliberately toward death: a cigarette, though she hasn't smoked for a decade. She and her mother discussed the details. Her mother had read Derek Humphry's *Final Exit*, a handbook on suicide for those who are terminally ill; over time, she had acquired enough pills to assure her own exit; and Neal had also checked with an unrelated physician to learn the proper dosage for someone who was not a hale and hearty person. Neal's brothers were not informed about their mother's plans, though one said after the death that he'd figured out that Neal had helped their mother and was glad that she could do it, for he could not. Neal says, "My mother knew how to do it; she had the supplies. But I told her, 'Mom, I know you want to tell people that you're checking out, and you want to say goodbye in an obvious way. But if you do that, you will be stopped. So you're either willing to do this, or we can do other things.' But she was determined." Neal then told her mother that she should do as much of the work as she possibly could, so that Neal could keep a discreet distance. She says, "I just really didn't know what was going to happen, so I was anxious to get it done, to get it done *right,* and get out of town. Maybe this was illegal. I didn't have any problems with the moral aspects of the situation, but I didn't know what other consequences might be. I would feel fear for this new territory that we were creating, and I'd have to tell myself that this is about her, this is for her, and that I could deal with whatever you've got after it's over.

"We had a wonderful three-day relationship. We fought. We played gin. We laughed. We saw friends. She saw babies and giggled and laughed, and she cried a little about aspects of family issues that were never going to be resolved. She ate forbidden foods and just had a wonderful party. Time took on a totally different aspect during those three days—we were so in the Now. It was eternal, what we were doing.

"Then, the method that she used was that she had an amazing collection of Nembutal. The way *Final Exit* talks about it is that first you drink tea and eat toast, then take a few of the pills with vodka, which was fun for her because it had been a long time since she'd had a drink, being diabetic. And when you find yourself getting sleepy, you would have taken some of the powder out of a lot of the pills and put them into a pudding. Just before you fall asleep, you eat that pudding."

Thursday evening arrived. Neal stayed with her mother till about 1 A.M. and went to bed after taking a Nembutal because she was too exhausted and wound up to go to sleep easily. At 4 A.M.

she awoke and went to her mother's room. Her mother lay on the floor amid a great spillage of pills. Neal will never know exactly what happened but surmises that, dropping the pills, her mother had left the bed to get them but could not rise again. She had achieved her intent and done it alone. But it's clear that she didn't want to be totally alone at the end. She wanted the fighting and card games, friends and laughter. "There was joy in her," Neal says. Her mother was sure that after death there was a place to go and that it held the great comfort of love. She had indeed gone to see what her sister Jean was up to.

Somehow, amid the cold details of gathering up furniture and her mother's other possessions all in the short space of twenty-four hours, Neal found that she was angry, realizing that nothing had been done to memorialize her mother. So she and a friend got on the phone. "We called all the people we knew of who had mingled in Mother's life in the final years. We told them that if you want to do something, if you feel incomplete, come to Mother's apartment at two o'clock. Maybe twenty people showed up. We sat in a circle on a rug, no furniture whatever, and I found a poem in Mother's Bible, a poem about dying and saying goodbye." Neal read the poem and found solace. Her mother was cremated and her ashes spread on the beach at Aunt Jean's oceanfront place, a reconnection to all that is timeless.

Before I leave, I ask Neal if she thinks human life is intrinsically sacred. "I have a sense that all life is sacred," she says. "Absolutely every bit of it is astoundingly miraculous in its endurance and fragility. That life occurs in a two-mile bubble on top of a planet and comes in so many varieties—there's something incredibly sacred about it. But I'm no more sacred than a tree. No, I don't think of human life as any more sacred than a dog's. One of my favorite quotes, I don't know who said it, is that when we come to think of nature as a community instead of a commodity, we will mature." I tell her that the concept comes from the great naturalist and conservationist Aldo Leopold.

It's worth mentioning that Derek Humphry, author of Neal's mother's handbook *Final Exit,* helped his first wife, Jean, die after her breast cancer had metastasized into her bones. He recounted the experience in *Jean's Way,* a book published in 1978. The experience propelled him into advocacy of death by choice, and in 1980 he and his second wife founded the Hemlock Society, an organization that aims to provide specific information to terminally ill people who wish to die. *Final Exit: The Practicalities of Self-Deliverance and Assisted Suicide for the Dying* was first published in 1981, became a bestseller, and has since been several times revised and updated. The contents are an omnium-gatherum, ranging from making the decision to die and shopping for a physician who will help to various methods of what Humphry terms "self-deliverance"—a drug overdose, a plastic bag, starvation, and carbon monoxide generated by an automobile. Among other things, an appendix contains the text of Oregon's Death with Dignity Act and a general form for a durable health-care power of attorney (DPA). My edition of the book is printed in large type, an aid to those of us with failing eyesight. Sales of *Final Exit* continue to be brisk. Humphry has used royalties from this blockbuster to help fund ballot initiatives on assisted suicide in California, Washington, and Oregon. He is now president of the Euthanasia Research and Guidance Organization, known emphatically as ERGO! (exclamation point theirs). The book, speaking privately to the desperate, points to a need to reexamine public policy on end-of-life matters.

A harrowing story comes to me in part from a woman I'll call Ellen, who was present at her mother's planned suicide, and in part from a mutual friend, who has known Ellen for more than fifty years. Ellen writes, giving me permission to say "another person you know witnessed her mother's death-by-choice, that the mother used drugs that affected her lungs, already severely compromised by chronic obstructive pulmonary disease, to bring about her demise. The mother had planned all her life to end her own life and not leave this most important event to chance. When she decided the time had come, she called family members to gather 'round, she carried out her plan, and they saw her through. She was utterly admirable—courageous and kind—to the end." But I learn through our mutual friend that the event did not go smoothly. Ellen's mother's illness kept her wheelchair-bound and in need of caregivers. And a caregiver knew of the decision to die. More than that, she knew its date. So, when the pills were taken, the caregiver called the authorities to say that her patient was dying and in need of being saved from murder. Ellen's mother died with strangers peering through the windows and pounding on the door. When entry was finally gained, Ellen's mother—admirable, generous, and kind—was dead. She had planned her death and attained it in the presence of people whom she loved, who loved her in return.

For many people who are close kin to someone ill and dying, the kind of death that Neal's and Ellen's mothers chose is not an option. They resist death with all the strength that body and soul can command, and if the thought arises that they might help speed a death, they push it away horrified, for life is sacrosanct, no matter that it may be riddled with debility or pain. I have come across several accounts in which family members have made a conscious decision to support life in the face of the most extreme adversity, to sustain breath until it ceases naturally. They intervene in treatment, but only on the side of life, the patient's lungs filling and heart pumping. But what is natural and what is not? I have found two stories that illustrate the difficulties, challenging and at the same time nebulous, of making that determination.

Philosopher Kathleen Dean Moore, who teaches in Oregon and writes winningly about elemental forces, like storms and rivers, and creatures, like the vocally acrobatic canyon wren and the huge Prometheus moth with see-all eyes on its wings, tells about these aspects of nature in her book *Holdfast: At Home in the Natural World*. There, she also recounts the story of her father's death. She traveled to her father's house, a thousand miles from home, where he lay dying with his longtime friend, his doctor, standing by. Of the two, she writes, "These were pragmatic, Depression-raised men, problem-solvers. If they were dying in pain, they wanted the dying to be quick, and then everyone could get on to other things. The doctor and I were both sure that we knew what my father wanted." Though he could not speak and his eyes were shut, her father was clearly in pain, sometimes breathing harshly, sometimes crying out. The doctor had not taken it upon himself to administer medicine that would alleviate the pain, for it would also shorten the little life remaining to his friend. Not just shorten his life but kill him then and there. But as his daughter, Kathleen Dean Moore could say Yes, could give her father final respite from all discomfort.

"Mercy killing is an enormous act," she writes. "It's a Promethean act, dangerous and proud—for better or for worse, stealing fire from the gods. It is beyond ethical categories. It is beyond laws and two signatures and review panels. Nothing requires it. Nothing justifies it. Greater than justice, it is an act of mercy, an act of love. It's a wrong that cannot be forgiven, a sharp-eyed, hard-beaked eagle tearing at Prometheus's immortal liver. It's the greatest gift one person can give another, a gift of stupendous love."

In writing about laws and signatures, she refers to the legislation sanctioning physician-assisted suicide in her home state, Oregon. But in her father's state, there are no such provisions. Her dilemma is cruel: that to say yes to the double effect, also known as terminal sedation, is not justified, is indeed an outright wrong, but one that at the same time constitutes an act of mercy and love. She says no. I cannot help wondering, however, if the issue was confused by the use of the word "killing." But patently, unlike Neal's mother and Jessamyn West's sister, her father could not make decisions for himself. Nonetheless, even knowing what he would have wanted, she clearly feels that saying yes was not an option. That mythic eagle would have torn at her conscience daily.

The story of Lucette Lagnado and her mother is of another order altogether. Ms. Lagnado's story, headlined "Mercy Living," appeared on the editorial page of *The Wall Street Journal* in January, 1995. In it she recounts taking her mother out of the nursing home in which the family had placed her and bringing her to Ms. Lagnado's apartment, where she finally died. The care was intensive: electric hospital bed, feeding pump, oxygen cylinders, bandages and syringes, respirator, round-the-clock nurses. Mother and daughter received visitors infrequently, for only a few people had been told about their way of life. "I dared not breathe a word about my living arrangement," Lucette Lagnado writes. "The few times I had attempted to describe what I was doing, I encountered bewilderment and, often, disapproval. This is, after all, the age where mercy killing is increasingly de rigueur. For baby boomers facing the problem of aging parents, assisted suicide is a hot topic. Terms like 'quality of life' and 'death with dignity' have become a code for letting loved ones die with a clear conscience."

She cries out for taking the opposite tack: "What of those of us who opt for mercy living? Who long to cast a vote for a resolution in support of assisted survival?"

At home, her mother suffered a series of strokes and other medical crises that worsened her condition. She became aphasic. She could not move nor swallow nor, eventually, breathe without a respirator. The younger woman characterizes the elder as "the fighter, the one who, reduced to a point of extraordinary vulnerability, looked to me to be her champion." And she castigates "the battery of neurologists, cardiologists, gastroenterologists, and pulmonologists" needed for her mother's survival. They would indicate that her efforts were misplaced, at best. When one asked her if she thought her mother was really alive, she fled in tears. Then, there were legal battles so that her mother would be allowed to continue with home care. But a social worker did give support, and several doctors made frequent calls. Ms. Lagnado writes, "She returned their caring, whether by a flicker of a smile, a gaze or, when she could still talk, the single word she uttered when asked how she was feeling: 'OK.'" And Ms. Lagnado cites as another boon the fact that her mother's illness "was even good for the economy of New York" by granting a living wage and steady jobs to the caregivers. After two years at home, Lucette Lagnado's mother died.

Of the letters that *The Wall Street Journal* received, it printed two that lauded both the idea of mercy living and its sponsor, one that corrected the source of a quotation in the article, but none that disagreed. The story appalls me; it sends earthquakes of shuddering up and down my spine. Many questions go unanswered. Had Lucette Lagnado's mother ever discussed with her daughter her own wishes should she become gravely ill? Was Ms. Lagnado so repulsed by the idea of mercy killing—that word again, "killing"—that she could not examine the options for living, one of which would be life at all costs, and the other, life with comfort; that she could not distinguish between a natural process and one that is unnatural? Her story seems one of merciless living.

Mercy living—the experience of a college classmate and friend, Nancy, who has co-authored two textbooks on literacy and only recently retired from teaching at the university level, truly transforms this idea into reality. Like Lucette Lagnado, Nancy took her own mother, Ruth, from a nursing facility and brought her home to her condominium in Orlando, Florida. She says that she and her mother had chatted from time to time for several years about the undesirability of being kept alive by tubes and machines. "So," Nancy says, "we filled out that piece of paper that states clearly one does not want tube feeding or hydration. She was still active, attending church, walking every morning, doing crossword puzzles, reading—a good time to have made the no-tube feeding decision." But as Ruth aged, she began to fail. She was eighty-eight years old, frail, and suffering from congestive heart failure, and she'd begun having episodes in which her blood pressure would drop and she'd lose consciousness. One day, when Nancy, then in her late fifties, was ready to take her mother to a doctor's appointment, her mother sat in a chair and said that she didn't feel well enough to go. Nancy describes what happened when she tried to help her mother to her feet. "She went rigid, eyes rolled back, mouth drawn in rictus. I thought she had died and, while horrified, some part of me thought, Good, she's gone, fast and without fuss—just like she'd like. I eased her to the floor, and she rallied a bit. I called the doctor, who had me call 911. She went into the hospital and then transferred to a nursing home."

The nursing home never gave Nancy a clear diagnosis. She was told that her mother was simply "failing to thrive." And Ruth's chart also noted senile dementia, though her mind was still alert, if somewhat faded. When Nancy challenged the finding of dementia, the doctor explained that it was always put on a chart for insurance purposes. He also said that Ruth seemed to be unable to answer the nurses' questions. Nancy snorts. "Of course, without her hearing aids in she couldn't hear them. But at the nursing home, Mother continued to be much as she had been for months. She was a compliant patient, always sweet to the aides, never complaining. She ate practically nothing, but lack of appetite was nothing new. They measured input and output, however, and told me that soon they would have to order tube feeding. I protested, showing them the paper indicating that she didn't want that, ever. But they said if I wanted to leave her there, I'd have to agree to the tube feeding on the grounds that the nursing home didn't allow people to starve. That made some sense from their viewpoint, but I couldn't see how they could do something to her she clearly didn't want done. I asked what the alternative was. They said, 'You can find someplace else for her or take her home.' So I brought her home."

The reason that the nursing home refused to keep Ruth unless she was intubated is that nursing homes everywhere are running scared. Hospitals and doctors accept the virtues of palliative care, but nursing homes often don't because of the all-too-real possibility that they will be accused by both the media and patients' families of elder-abuse and negligence. Oh, Mrs. X is being starved, Mr. Y has bedsores, and it's all the fault of a nursing home's insufficient care—this is a not-uncommon perception of the way things are but shouldn't be. The perception is erroneous. The truth is that many of these people are wasting away from terminal diseases. They are dying.

Nancy recalls that the day she brought her mother home was Groundhog Day, a Friday. A neighbor helped carry Ruth upstairs to Nancy's second-floor condominium. The next day a nurse from the visiting nurses agency came to evaluate the new patient. When Nancy asked if the decision not to allow tube feeding was the right one, the nurse said, "Absolutely. If she were sixty or even seventy, tube feeding might very well be the right thing to do while she gets stronger. But at her age, and in her condition, it will just go straight through her. It won't really supply nourishment and certainly not result in her recovery." And the nurse told Nancy that her mother was probably not going to rally, that a return to good health was unlikely, and the most that tube feeding could accomplish would be to prolong her life for another week or two. Then she looked Nancy in the eye, shook her hand, and said, "You are doing the right thing. Let her go." To this day, Nancy is grateful for the strength given her by this support.

She readied herself to care for her mother as long as she would live. Ruth wanted to return to her own house; she talked wistfully about sitting at her kitchen table with the breezes blowing. But she acquiesced when Nancy told her that for now it was good to be where Nancy could best help her. Furniture was acquired to make the stay more comfortable: a used wheelchair, a portable commode placed in the living room next to the chair in which the older woman usually sat, and a lightweight chair with an adjustable back and an ottoman which could be put anywhere in the house to give her a vista from any window.

"I offered her food and drink frequently," Nancy says, "but didn't nag. I never told her that she had to eat if she wanted to get well. This was a woman of sound mind despite her failing body. I wouldn't treat her like a child. I fixed meals I knew she liked. She would eat one or two tiny bites, then tell me how delicious it was but she'd finish it later. After she died, my refrigerator was filled with custard cups carefully covered with Saran wrap for 'later.'

She asked for a drink often but seldom swallowed more than one or two sips. I think her mouth was dry, and she didn't really feel thirst but just wanted moisture. She dozed most of the time but called me many times during the night because she was uncomfortable and didn't have the strength to change position. Within two or three days, I was exhausted and beginning to wonder how I could possibly continue to live this way, caring for her, never sleeping through the night, teaching my classes at the university."

The visiting nurses continued to come. One was present when Nancy's mother suffered an episode of plummeting blood pressure. Nancy was advised that Ruth didn't have long to live and that it would be good to get a do-not-resuscitate order so that Nancy could just call the funeral home right away when her mother died. Nancy worried that she wouldn't know when her mother was dead, but she was instructed by the nurses to call one of them, for they were able to make a pronouncement of death. Under no circumstances should Nancy call 911, for, in the absence of a do-not-resuscitate order, a rescue squad was legally obliged, like it or not, to do everything possible to bring her back to life.

Nancy's mother stayed in bed much of the time, though she made a great effort to sit up because a nurse had told her that she should. Once, as Nancy left her room, Ruth sang out, "Goodbye!" When Nancy said that she was just going into the other room, her mother smiled and said that she knew that but thought that she herself might go somewhere. Nancy laughed and asked, "Where?" Ruth pointed at the ceiling and said, "Upstairs." Nancy says that she was puzzled at the time but understood later that she meant she knew that she would soon die—and that it was all right. Her faith was strong; she believed in a life after death.

On Thursday evening, Nancy's daughter came to stay with her grandmother so that Nancy could attend a concert. The next day, February 9, was beautiful—warm, sunny, open windows.

Nancy sat behind her mother and lifted her slowly so that the blood pressure could adjust, but Ruth was unable to sit up by herself. For a long time, Nancy held her mother in her arms as she slipped in and out of consciousness. Then, "Suddenly, her entire insides let go. Everything just emptied out. She seemed hardly aware of it." Nancy washed her mother, put her into a clean nightgown, and changed the bed. The visiting nurses were called. A cousin came over to sit with Nancy and her mother. They held Ruth's hands and talked as they watched her chest rise and fall slightly. "Then it stopped. That was it. She died. It was just under a week after I'd brought her home from the nursing home. It was very peaceful."

She adds, "I'd done the right thing. She was two weeks shy of her eighty-ninth birthday, so one can hardly say that she died too soon. The image of that beautiful last morning is comforting to me still." Mercy living, yes. Though from the nursing home's point of view Nancy had allowed her mother to starve, the older woman's wishes had been honored, and she died amid love. Like Neal's mother, she went gently into that good night, and, until the very last moment, she was not alone.

Can this be called an assisted death? I think so, though of the tenderest sort. It was not a suicide but rather a death caused by omission. Tubes for water and food were not inserted. Nothing active was done to cause Nancy's mother's demise. Instead, the event was passive, in huge contrast to the wearying experience— keeping an old, terminally ill woman alive at all costs—related by Lucette Lagnado and to the violence perpetrated by the self-appointed Dr. Death.

IT'S WELL to take a brief look at the workings of Dr. Death, more formally known as Dr. Jack Kevorkian, a pathologist—a man trained to work with tissues and corpses, who was convicted in 1999 of second-degree murder. During a decade of activity, he helped at least 130 people kill themselves. For his first clients he provided a machine, which he called the Thanitron or Mercitron, which administered a narcotic followed by a lethal dose of potassium chloride. When he lost his license to practice medicine in Michigan and so lost access also to prescription drugs, he resorted to carbon monoxide as the means for a client to commit suicide. Tried four times for assisting a suicide, he had three acquittals, while the fourth attempt resulted in a mistrial. But he was adjudged guilty of murder for the last of his clients, Thomas Youk, a victim of amyotrophic lateral sclerosis (ALS), better known as Lou Gehrig's disease. Youk was then too paralyzed by his sickness to swallow medication. So Kevorkian injected Youk with a lethal drug and made a videotape of the act. Then, in a fit of almost unbelievable arrogance, he aired the tape on television. The judge who sentenced him said, "You had the audacity to go on national television, show the world what you did and dare the system to stop you. Well, sir, consider yourself stopped." The line from passive assistance to active euthanasia had been crossed.

But the sad fact that Kevorkian flourished for so long at helping people, not all of them terminally ill, to end their lives points to a pair of social needs that are not well addressed. The first is the desirability of providing far better medical care, so that people who are seriously ill and even dying may be made comfortable both in body and spirit. Modern medicine can, in a host of ways, transform life into something worth living. It can, for example, keep pain at bay, and relieve depression, which often triggers thoughts of dying as the only possible surcease. For those in their last illness, hospice organizations offer many services from bathing patients to comforting them and their families. Then, factors causing stress may be identified and remedied, and visiting nurses offer treatment at home. Sometimes the simple provision of companionship—a person, a pet—is enough to turn darkness into light.

As for the second need, Kevorkian serves as a gruesome warning signal that it is imperative for our society to reexamine the bioethical issues relating to maintaining life (something we like to think about) and to death and dying (something we relegate to the remotest gulag in our minds). It is not necessary to condone Kevorkian's acts to recognize that a formidable gulf exists in America between the often case-bound rigors of the law and the possibilities inherent in medical and technological discovery. In light of current knowledge, the time has surely come to recognize that the idea of the sanctity of human life is sometimes just that—an idea—and that it may bear no resemblance to reality.

It is, however, an idea possessed of ferocious power in the Western world, an idea given weight by the Christian belief that man is formed in the image of God. Our view has thus been homocentric, with other life seen as revolving around and subservient to humankind. This article of faith now seems akin to the notion of geocentricity—that earth was at the core of the universe, with all other heavenly bodies orbiting around it. Copernicus and Galileo began the scientific work that put earth in its rightful place as a planet in a solar system that wheels around the sun. Science in the person of Darwin has also delivered a stunning blow to the idea of a huge community of life that wheels around humankind. And the unriddling of the human genome has added its force to the dislodgment. The 1.6 percent difference in DNA between human beings and chimpanzees is less than the 2.3 percent between chimpanzees and gorillas, though a study published in 2002 reports a 5 percent difference between humankind and chimps. Whatever the percentage, the line between who is human and who is not becomes blurred. When I talked with Neal, she gave me her belief that all life—not just human life—is worthy of respect; with this statement, she gives voice to a fairly broad change of opinion in America. An ancient aphorism attributed to Hippocrates sounds in my mind: The souls of living creatures are the same, although their bodies differ. How is it possible today to view sanctity of human life as a governing principle?

And this is the ethical issue, the prickly, sensibility-roiling, outcry-provoking issue that is addressed by the legalization of physician-assisted suicide in Oregon and euthanasia in both the Netherlands and Sweden. The difference between assisted suicide and euthanasia, a classical Greek word that means "good death," is that the former denotes a death that occurs when a patient takes legally prescribed drugs, while the latter is a death that results from a lethal injection given by someone else. The distinction rests between intention on the one hand and action on the other. As a Web site on euthanasia puts it:

> 'Assisting' suicide in the sense of general provision
> of info on how to commit suicide is probably not
> illegal anywhere—except in France—especially
> if it is not directly and knowingly given to a person
> about to commit suicide. 'Assisting' in the sense of
> being present varies from area to area in whether it
> is against the law.
>
> 'Assisting' in the sense of directly providing the
> means (as did Dr. Kevorkian, or as provided by Ore-
> gon's Death with Dignity Act) is what is generally
> so controversial.

In the 1990s and early 2000s, proposals to legalize physician-assisted suicide were put before the voters in several states, among them California, Maine, Michigan, Oregon, and Washington. Only Oregon's voters approved, and by a narrow margin, a 1994 referendum to legalize physician-assisted suicide. But the courts blocked the law from taking effect for the next three years. During that time, several groups sought to have the law declared unconstitutional, but the Supreme Court of the United States refused to hear the case, leaving it up to Oregonians to decide yea or nay. On November 4, 1997, a ballot initiative to repeal the law was defeated by a walloping 60 percent to 40 percent, and Oregon's Death with Dignity Act took effect. This is not the only time in recent years that Oregon has been a pioneer. In 1997, state government began funding a program to aid not only the parents of disabled young children but also the parents of disabled children who have reached adulthood.

Oregon's Death with Dignity Act specifies, among other provisions, that the patient requesting "a prescription to end his or her life in a humane and dignified manner" must be at least eighteen years old and also able to offer proof of residence in the state of Oregon, like a driver's license, voter's registration, or a state tax return for the most recent tax year. In other words, no nonresidents need apply. And the act, a far cry from Dr. Kevorkian's rather casual approach, is filled with safeguards. The request for help in ending life, in oral and written form, must be made three times, with a fifteen-day waiting period between the first request and the last. Both an attending physician and a consulting physician must certify that the patient is not only competent but also facing death within six months. The patient will be advised to have another person present when the prescribed medication is taken and cautioned sternly not to take it in a public place. If depression or other mental problems leading to impaired judgment are discerned, the request will be denied and the patient referred to counseling. The patient must also be capable of self-administration of the medication. If, as with Thomas Youk, the ability to swallow has been lost, the doctors will not act. In every case, the patient is to be advised of alternatives, such as hospice care and pain management. In no case will preemptive suicide—a suicide designed to avoid future events rather than deal with present illness—be condoned.

Why do Oregonians accept such a law, and not, say, Michiganders, Californians, Washingtonians, or residents of Maine? I can only offer a rough guess. Polls show that the Western states are more open to the idea of doctors providing patients with the means to die. The reason may be the very urge that thrust people westward into the unknown. Riding in Conestoga wagons, rushing for gold, they expanded the geographic frontier. By extension, Oregon's law expands a bioethical frontier. A study published in the *Journal of the American Medical Association* finds, however, that ninety percent of the Oregonians who ask their doctors to help them die later change their minds.

The Netherlands provides still another, more profound expansion of the frontier. On April 1, 2002, euthanasia and assisted suicide—both the active and passive provisions of medical aid in dying—achieved the status of law (Sweden followed suit later in the same year). Both forms had long existed in the country of dikes, wooden shoes, and squeaky clean farms, and their practice was hardly *sub rosa*, something carried out in back alleys under cover of night. Mercy killing was considered a criminal offense but one that was completely defensible, for a court could be asked to decide whether a doctor who had assisted at a death had experienced a conflict between his oath to preserve life and his duty to relieve suffering. By 1984, the Royal Dutch Medical Association had issued a statement describing the conditions under which voluntary euthanasia should be permissible—voluntary meaning that a mentally competent person had requested help. The conditions were these: that only a doctor should administer euthanasia; that the patient, expressing a desire to die, made a clear request for help; that the patient's decision be informed and freely made; that the patient's pain and suffering be intolerable and without hope of improvement; that no other measures to alleviate suffering be available; and that the doctor not only exercise all due caution in deciding to participate but get a second opinion from another physician. In 1993, the Dutch parliament passed a law that came close to regularizing euthanasia by requiring physicians to report instances to a prosecutor, who could then determine whether there had been a true conflict between preserving life and bringing it to a dignified end. The practice of euthanasia was not common then, but it was far from being thought of as an act beyond the pale. Today, the statutes legalizing and furnishing guidelines for assisted suicide and euthanasia are in place. It should be noted that many of the deaths officially listed as occurring from euthanasia do not stem from the active injection of a lethal drug but rather from the passive withdrawal of life-support from people who are slipping quickly, inexorably out of this world. The overall experience in the Netherlands may not be open to duplication in the United States, for the Dutch live in a welfare state, in which no one goes without medical care. But it does show that traditional thinking can be transformed by taking a new look at reality.

It's worth mentioning that, since 1942, Switzerland has permitted legal euthanasia for Swiss citizens who have a life-expectancy of only two or three weeks. Sixty years later, the policy has mutated so that assisted suicide is legally available to people who suffer from a wide variety of unbearable conditions, ranging from terminal illnesses to intolerable mental anguish, defined in a *Wall Street Journal* article as "a musician, for example, who had gone deaf." Safeguards are in place under Swiss law: People who ask for euthanasia must be rational and able to take the lethal drug themselves, and three witnesses must be present, including a health-care professional. But in 1998, an organization called Dignitas—the Latin word for "dignity"—came into being, and under its ministrations, not only the Swiss but citizens from other countries are helped to end their lives.

The very idea of a doctor giving passive or active help so that a patient will die excites vigorous, not to mention heated, cries for and against. Nor is it just assisted suicide that creates a roaring rumpus of argument. Some people decry the administration of palliative drugs for pain that result in hastening death. But the Supreme Court of the United States has issued decisions speaking to the matter. Noting that dying may well subject someone to unmanageable hurting, Justice Sandra Day O'Connor has pointed out that "the laws do not *force* a dying person to undergo that kind of pain." And the Court has ever made a distinction between helping someone to commit suicide and the right of a patient to refuse life-saving treatment. The difference lies "between letting a patient die and making a patient die." Assisted suicide, in the Court's opinion, is not to be equated with "the withdrawing or withholding of treatment, and from the provision of palliative treatments or other medical care that risk fatal side effects."

Laws like those of Oregon and the Netherlands that give sanction to assisted suicide stir even more passionate debate. Advocates and opponents on both sides include doctors, lawyers and legislators, theologians, and terminally ill patients. All are convinced that they hold the moral high ground. The proponents argue that a person who is dying should have the right to decide about the moment and the means of death. Then, if someone declares life to have become a constant misery or to lack all meaning, no legislature or court, no medical group or facility should act coercively to prevent death. In light, also, of the fact that many doctors, like the friend of Kathleen Dean Moore's father, are willing to administer lethal drugs, laws and regulations, rather than proscriptions, are needed to provide guidelines to a practice that is not uncommon, though it is not widely or openly acknowledged. And the sanctioning of physician-assisted suicide is seen as a merciful response that gives a dying person a chance to die a planned death or to die naturally, as that person so chooses. Opponents cite the slippery slope—the difficulty, that is, in discerning the point at which compassionate assistance slides willy-nilly into murder. They state, too, that doctors are bound by the Hippocratic oath never to take a patient's life or to help in doing so. Thus, to participate in assisted suicide would be to violate professional principles and standards. And they believe that the safeguards provided in proposed laws on assisted suicide would, without doubt, leave patients vulnerable to decisions made by others. Opponents also believe that instances of assisted suicide would be more common in families who have no insurance and cannot otherwise afford the costs of medical care for a dying member. And, goodness knows, like my mother and Neal's, people as they age often express a fear of becoming a burden to their families. So, opponents claim that families exhausted in body and mind by caring for a dying person might all too easily push that person into requesting a death that comes by design rather than by nature.

Who is right, and who is wrong? The bioethics dealing with assisted suicide, along with laws, judicial decisions, and professional standards, are in a state of flux, as is the Hippocratic oath, which comes in almost as many modern versions as there are medical schools, both here and abroad. Nor do these come-lately oaths faithfully follow the original; nowadays, for example, most do not abjure having sexual relations with patients, and the small percentage that have retained some of this part of the oath have eliminated the Hippocratic descriptions of the patients not to be seduced as male or female, free or slave. More notably, some contemporary versions do not repeat, or come near repeating, the classical injunction not to prescribe lethal drugs or to give advice that may lead to a patient's death; they vow instead to give all such matters due consideration. Oath, laws, and standards are being pushed from the old familiar rut into unknown territory. Many of the pros and cons have never undergone the rigors of testing. And testing, of course, is controversial, and not just controversial but shunned, for lives are at stake, and also deaths. Even with safeguards in place, laws dealing with assisted suicide and euthanasia are not fail-safe. Just as there will always be poachers, songbird killers, and otherwise upstanding people who abandon unwanted kittens and pups, just as there will always be arsonists who put forests to the torch so that they can work as fire-fighters and pharmacists who dilute drugs so that they can maximize their profits, there will also be doctors who give non-voluntary lethal injections. It needs to be asked, however, just who is harmed when someone expresses a desire to die; if no one is harmed, then there is no possible reason not to respect a request for death. As John Stuart Mill, the nineteenth-century British philosopher, has said in regard to the role of government in human affairs, "The only purpose for which power can be rightfully exercised over any member of a civilised community, against his will, is to prevent harm to others. His own good, either physical or moral, is not a sufficient warrant." In the end, one issue emerges as paramount: Who is in charge? The dying person? The family, however exhausted? The doctor? Politicians courting votes? An icily impersonal bureaucracy?

I reflect on the accounts that I've read and the stories told to me. The tellers are all people solidly ensconced in the ranks of the America's middle class. Though the sampling is so small that it can hold no statistical value, every portion of it illustrates compassion on the part of the living, even the stubborn, almost bellicose compassion of Lucette Lagnado. And it's already been said that none of these people flay themselves with the abrasive lash of guilt. Instead, they believe with all their hearts that they have taken the right course in helping someone they love to live and die. For, death is a part of life, though, granted, its final part. Death, eventually, is all that's left.

COULD I HAVE helped my mother die? Could I have played the role of Betty Rollin and Jessamyn West, of Neal and Ellen? I think so, but the test does not come.

Do Not Resuscitate

> It is impossible that anything so natural, so
> necessary, and so universal as death, should
> ever have been designed by Providence as an
> evil to mankind.
>
> —Jonathan Swift, "Thoughts on Religion"

AT FIRST, Sarah slips downhill imperceptibly. January: She comes home from the rehabilitation center still able to concoct a jingle in the blink of an eye. She's in a wheelchair but can help the caregivers when they settle her in her recliner, bathe her, and put her to bed. Her appetite excels, and she can feed herself. She delights in her little white toy poodle, Muffin, who licks her hand and sits in her lap. Friends come often to visit, and sometimes, accompanied by one of the caregivers, she goes with them to an in-town restaurant or a country inn. Aphasia sometimes frustrates her. The main difficulty is left-side neglect. She has lost the ability to use her left eye, although the eye retains the power of sight, nor can the therapists who come to the townhouse for continuing rehab sessions bring it back into play. She writes letters and jots notes but only on the right side of a page. She gets news from visitors, for reading a newspaper—having to move her head or shift the paper from right to left one column at a time—is no longer something she can do with ease. Yet, her metamorphosis into a rainbow is nowhere in sight.

February and March: She is connected to the larger world by more than visitors. Deciding to upgrade the business power of attorney that she has given me, she summons her attorneys. When the upgrade has been accomplished, one of them invites her to call him at any time if she has questions. She looks at him, smiles brightly, and says, "No questions. Oh, I might call to ask you what day it is." She knows full well that she is making a joke.

April and May: She begins to lose the ability to help the caregivers with transfers. Spells of being tongue-tied come more frequently. She cannot easily call her little dog but summons the animal when she sees it with a wiggle of her fingers. Yet her friends, who visit frequently, bringing flowers or good things to eat, say with an incredulous amazement that she seems, against all odds, to be *happy*. I think that she is indeed happy, sitting like a rock in the middle of a stream with life in full flow around her.

Summer: Sarah's air of happiness, contentment, and well-being continues. There is, however, a cloud that sometimes shadows it. She wants to walk. And she asks the caregivers to help her. The very idea terrifies me, for if she were to fall, her old, osteoporotic bones would likely break. Or, as happens with advanced osteoporosis, a bone could break first and cause the fall. Nonetheless, a contraption is rigged in her sitting room—two railings made stable by a sheet of plywood. I never see her use it but imagine that the caregivers may well have hoisted her to her feet and placed her hands on the railings. The thing soon disappears. She still has considerable upper body strength, but her legs aren't willing to support her, much less to walk. This time she yields graciously to defeat.

September: With the waning of the year comes waning of body and mind. Sarah stops trying to write. The tongue-tied spells increase; her ability to communicate slips. The friends who used to invite her out for restaurant meals now come to visit her at home. It's clear that she enjoys the company and that she understands what people are saying even if she has great trouble responding. The aura of well-being continues for the most part.

October: not quite a year after the second stroke, the seizures begin. They are little seizures—petit mal seizures—not dramatic spasms. It is as if a switch has been flicked off in Sarah's brain. Her expression changes instantly from fairly lively interest in the world around her to puzzled frowns. Her eyes roam the room in search of—who knows what? She obviously does not see the caregivers or visitors or her little dog. But two minutes later, the switch turns on again, the smiles and calm demeanor return. These small but furious electrical storms occur as often as once or twice every thirty minutes. In early November, we take her to a neurologist, who prescribes the anticonvulsant Dilantin to prevent the seizures. Peace returns to Sarah's countenance and, more important, to her brain.

What should we do if she suffers yet another stroke? How should we respond? Because she has told me, though in another life, that she would not want to live as she now must—speechless, immobile, incontinent, increasingly confused, completely dependent—I think that she should be allowed to die, to attain at last her rainbowhood. Without hospitalization and the operation to relieve the hematoma, she would have died shortly after the second stroke. But she has lived—to what avail? The very idea that she might be snatched back once again from the brink of eternity horrifies me. It is not enough, however, for me to think such things. My wishes, even though I believe that they reflect hers, are not sufficient to stay the hands of family, caregivers, doctors, and the rescue squad.

TIMOR MORTIS CONTURBAT ME: the fear of death roils me. It has always roiled human consciousness. We do not like to contemplate our finitude. To do so makes us so uncomfortable that we hide from it or run; we tuck it deeply away amid other unsettling, unwanted impedimenta in the cellars and attics of our minds. In America particularly, we do our damnedest to seek a cure for mortality. Beware of biological extinctions, for example, because when we lose a fragment of life on earth, we may well lose, for all we know, a vital, healing principle that once existed in the lost venom or the gone-forever sap. Consider, too, the pro-life movement: All life is sacred—as long as it's human. And heaven forfend that we, earth's representatives of the Divine, do not avail ourselves of the latest gizmos and medications. The poet William Butler Yeats identified the two great topics of humankind as death and love. Once upon a time, in Victorian days, to speak of death was commonplace, for death was taken for granted, while talk of sexuality and sexual love was taboo. Today, matters have been turned topsy-turvy: obsessed by sex, we shove the very idea of death, not to mention the reality, into the farthest, dimmest corner of our minds.

Yet, ineluctably, the time comes for each of us to die. There's no ducking the ultimate shutdown. The questions are: To what degree should life be extended or dying prolonged? And, how can any of us humanly judge that one life is worth laboring to save while another should go by the boards?

I look at my mother, wandering fitfully, fearfully in and out of comprehension. She is like a lost child. Because we have talked about her wishes at length, when she was vigorous and keen, I know without a doubt that she would not want to be as she is. She has no choices, though, given her present incapacity. But I do. I go about seeking a do-not-resuscitate order. She is so frail and ill that wrenching her back into life, should she suffer a third stroke or some other biological thunderbolt, would amount to renewing her lease on misery. I cannot help her as much as I'd like, but there's one thing that I am able to do—keep her from further indignities of helplessness. No need for resuscitation that would only allow her suffering to spin on unabated. Getting a DNR, however, turns out to be unexpectedly—inexcusably—difficult.

All fifty states have passed legislation that authorizes three potently useful advance medical directives that may be made by people unafraid to anticipate the inevitable: living will, durable health-care power of attorney (DPA), and DNR. This legislation is relatively recent. Before 1967, the concept of a living will did not exist; it was transformed into reality when California passed its Natural Death Act in 1976. DPAs came along later, legalized in forty states by 1987, and by all fifty in 1992. The three advance directives speak in different ways to end-of-life issues. A living will outlines in general the kind of treatment that you'd prefer in your last days, from taking advantage of all special measures to using none at all. It's drawn up when you're in full possession of your senses but comes into play only when you're diagnosed with a terminal illness and have fewer than six months to live. Though it may name someone—a family member, a friend—who can do some gentle pushing and shoving, it does not allow that person to speak for you if you cannot do it yourself. But even if you have stated your wishes in a living will and put it into the hands of your doctor, even if you are compos mentis when you fall seriously ill, it may well be that the health-care professionals pay the

document no heed. A 1995 study found that "there were no differences in health outcome or medical treatment between those
who had signed advance directives and those who hadn't."

A friend—I'll call her Margaret—tells me about her mother,
who suffered a heart attack at the age of eighty-six. A rescue
squad, summoned by calling 911, resuscitated her, and she was
then hospitalized. When Margaret reached the hospital after an
international flight, she found that her mother was intubated for
feeding and was wearing an oxygen mask. She says, "We explained to the doctors about her living will and how she didn't
want any heroic measures. This is difficult for them because they
are in the business of saving lives. They tried to put a tube down
her throat, but she bit the doctor's finger!" In the hospital, Margaret's mother suffered another heart attack and was again resuscitated, even though it had been clearly stated that the elderly
woman did not want to be brought back. Oxygen mask covering
her nose and mouth, she lay there unconscious for a while but
waked early the next morning. Margaret says that her mother was
miserable, tugging weakly at the mask, wanting it off, and she has-
tened to get a nurse to take it off. But the nurse said that the mask
could not be removed, doctor's orders. Was it possible to use a
lighter, more comfortable mask? Margaret didn't want her mother
to die but also found it wrenching to see her mother's misery.
After a long argument, someone did come to put on a lighter mask
that allowed the old woman to speak. Nor was that the end of professional interference. "Mom was in great distress," Margaret
says. "They removed her catheter, but her heart medications were
making liquids pass right through her, and no one would answer
her call bell in time to help her to the commode." So, Margaret
stayed in the room to escort her mother when the need arose. But
with physical therapy and medicines, the older woman was able

to return home in time for Christmas. Two months later, she suffered another heart attack. This time, when Margaret talked with the doctor, everyone was in accord that the time had come to let her die peacefully.

A living will—my mother named me in hers and years later signed an affidavit to reaffirm its contents. I gave a copy to her first primary-care physician—I'll call him Dr. Douglas—and then, after he had terrified her, to his replacement.

AUGUST, one year and nine months after the second stroke: terror comes after one of the caregivers finds a lump in Sarah's breast. When Dr. D. makes a house call to examine it, he speaks casually and within Sarah's hearing to a family member. They discuss at length the possibility of a mastectomy. Sarah, possessed by panic, loses all ability to understand and becomes extremely irrational for the next two months, nor are we able to explain to her that, because we do not know the nature of the lump, a mastectomy is not now on the agenda, though a biopsy would give us that information. "Cut off my breast," she whimpers, "cut off my breast."

Her out-of-bounds response, her panic, is known as a "catastrophic reaction," an overreaction of the most extreme sort. *The 36-Hour Day,* one of the pitifully few books on dementia written for a non-technical audience, defines it further: "We use the term *catastrophic reaction* to describe the behavior. The word *catastrophic* is used in a special sense; it does not mean that these occasions are necessarily very dramatic or violent." So it is the behavior of a demented person, not its stimulus, that is calamitous.

In our ignorance, we also respond catastrophically. We follow Dr. D.'s advice to submit Sarah to a stereotactic needle biopsy, rather than a surgical procedure or a less invasive aspiration of the lump with a needle after the lump has been manually located. On the surface, stereotaxis seems to be on the leading edge of technology. The site for the biopsy is established three-dimensionally, by height, width, and depth. This information is entered into a computer, which is then able to position the needle to take a sample from the appropriate place. The reality, as we discover, is that the procedure is neither simple nor kind.

Rosa, my brother Joe, and I go with her to the hospital, where she is given a mammogram, then wheeled into the room where the biopsy will take place. The room, in a trailer detached from the hospital proper and reached by a ramp, is almost medieval. Once we enter, a great door made of widely interwoven metal strips comes clanging down like a portcullis. Sarah shudders at the sound. We can see her struggle to understand what's happening. And she finds an answer. In a faint, fearful voice, she says, "Jail! Jail!" Much of the room is filled with a table akin to something you might find in a torture chamber. As I remember it, it is riddled with holes like Swiss cheese. Instructed by an aide, Rosa and Joe help Sarah up from her wheelchair and place her on the table belly down so that the afflicted breast can hang downward through a hole. The idea is that the doctor sitting beside this unholy contraption will have easier access to the part in question so that he can make a needle-aspiration as the computer directs. To begin with, he takes a long time coming, and after he finally arrives, he begins angling for her breast. Twenty minutes later, he has still not collected a sample. Computer be damned, the difficulty rises from thin, aged skin that slithers out of reach every time he aims for it. We finally pack up and go home with patience frazzled and nothing accomplished. The moral of the story is, of course, to learn as much as possible ahead of time so that a decision, yea or nay, can be reasonably made. It should have been apparent from the beginning to Dr. D. and the doctor who tried to perform the biopsy that Sarah was not a good candidate for stereotaxis. For nearly two months afterward, she is in a swivet, wildly fearful, talking of jail and a cut-off breast. The lump is still there the following March, though it has not grown larger. I make arrangements for her to go to my own surgeon for an out-patient aspiration. The lump, hallelujah, is not malignant. Indeed, it turns out to be a cyst.

IT IS A BOON to both of us that Sarah has given me the power to speak for her in a business power of attorney. My duties keep me driving up and down the road—a round trip of more than seven hundred miles at least once a month and sometimes more frequently—between her home in Virginia and mine in North Carolina, where the Chief and I live for the spring, summer, and most of the fall. The jobs entailed run the gamut from paying bills and filing federal and state tax returns to arbitrating difficulties among the trio of caregivers and conferring frequently with my own triumvirate of accountant, attorney, and banker. With the banker, I negotiate a line of credit, for her personal funds are running low. I also purchase health-care supplies for her caretakers and fill in when needed as her chauffeur to and from appointments with doctors and dentists. And I clear away the clutter that has accumulated in the course of two moves. A major project is sorting through box after box of my mother's belongings. When she came to her townhouse, the things that she did not immediately need were stashed in dozens of cardboard cartons and stored in the townhouse's basement. The assortment of stuff, the hodgepodge of gold and dross down there is boggling. Yellowing news clippings, torn travel brochures, and minutes of meetings held decades ago are mixed with some of my great-grandmother's silver and a silver stamp box bearing my grandmother Jannette's initials. Ten years of empty Christmas-card envelopes, saved for their addresses, and twenty years of rubber bands that once encircled the local newspaper (waste not, want not) mingle higgledy-piggledy with dozens of family photographs made over nearly a century and a half. I sort through every last carton, saving things possessed of value, throwing the rest away. For every five bags of trash taken to the dumpster, I salvage a shoebox of treasure. One family member, taking umbrage at the amount of stuff being thrown away, calls my sisters and brothers to tell them that I am throwing away pieces of their lives. The solution is to invite them all to help with the sorting and triage. No one accepts.

I will learn later that there is a formal name for the role I played: geriatric care manager. It is a recognized profession inhabited by people, variously trained in gerontology, nursing, social work, and counseling, who arrange for and supervise daily care. Their fees run from $40 to $95 an hour. The cost is not covered by Medicare or most health insurance, but many long-term-care policies will kick in with reimbursements for certain kinds of care at home. And professional GCMs have a trade association with a web site: the National Association of Geriatric Care Managers (www.caremanager.org). Some are certified by the National Academy of Certified Care Managers; some are not. But we who are necessary but nonprofessional GCMs receive our training and certification on the job and our reimbursement consists of occasional silver linings amid the tensions and hard work.

Because I can be Sarah's voice in matters of business, we are able to avoid some of the problems that not infrequently beset the elderly, even when they're rational. The proprietor of a local private home health-care agency reminds me that aging people often wait too long. They put off naming an advocate, a spokesperson, who is personally selected and can be trusted to abide by the nominator's wishes. Stashing mortality in a closet and shutting the door is not unnatural; we all do it. But the consequences may be severe. One of the agency's clients, a woman in her early nineties, though still quite capable of making informed decisions, has forfeited her independence to a middle-aged relative who moved in and immediately thereafter took over management of her affairs. In other words, an upstart staged a coup, and the rightful government was toppled without a hope of regaining power. It happens, too, that banks don't care who writes the signature on a check as long as the signed name matches that on the account. The lesson is, if you leave a vacuum, it will be filled but not necessarily by someone of your choosing.

BEWARE THE LIVING WILL. With one shining exception, it is not the best means for resolving end-of-life issues. It kicks in only when a physician foresees that death will occur within half a year. *Foresee* or *predict*—either is the right word for a haphazard art, akin to fortune-telling, holding a séance, and reading the auspices in entrails or tarot cards; it's an art as ambiguous as interpreting a prophesy from the Delphic oracle. For, it is well nigh impossible for a human being to pronounce with any certainty that there is a lead-time of six or fewer months to the hour of death. In addition, a living will means nothing to a rescue squad, whose duty is to preserve life come hell or high water, nor does its existence ensure that the signer will escape extraordinary medical interventions. All too often, doctors and nurses—advocates of life who wage war on death—will ignore it unless the family member or friend who may be named to speak for a dying person behaves like a dog that won't let go of a bone. It cannot officially appoint anyone to speak authoritatively on behalf of the patient, who may—or may not—be rational. Finally, with its six-month requirement, it is not designed to save anyone whose death may be far away, such as people in a persistent vegetative state, from merciless intervention. But hearing me dismiss the living will as a useful instrument, my own physician reminds me that it has one stellar virtue: writing it up stimulates conversations among family members and with doctors. Surely, anything that provokes constructive talk about personal views of death and dying—talk too often avoided—is not to be shunned but rather embraced.

The instrument that gives an advocate a clear, strong, legally recognized voice is the DPA, which designates both an agent and a successor, should the former become unable to act. It is far more inclusive than a living will. Most states accept every state's version of such a DPA, but if a version is not legally recognized in your state, it nonetheless gives family and physician clear guidance if you aren't able to make decisions on your own. Another lesson is given here: make every effort to get the DPA authorized by the state in which you live.

I look at my own DPA, which I signed in 1993, a year after my mother's first stroke. It was drawn up as an almost terrified response to my mother's lack of such an instrument. At seven single-spaced pages, it is indeed a comprehensive document. It allows my agent to consent to or refuse any kind of medical treatment; to have access to my medical records; to put me in a hospital, assisted-living facility, or nursing home, and also to take me out of such a place and bring me back to my own house; to hire and fire the support people who will care for me; and "to authorize any medication or procedure intended to relieve pain, even though such use may lead to physical damage or addiction or hasten the moment of my death." More than that, it informs my agent that I do not want my life prolonged nor do I wish life-sustaining treatment—like a respirator acting as a bellows pushing air into my lungs or a nose-to-stomach feeding tube—if the agent "believes that the burdens of the treatment outweigh the expected benefits." The key to constructing a successful DPA is naming agents who will keep the faith and do their best to abide by your directives. As is, the existence of my own DPA wraps me in comfort. It's on file with my doctor. More important, it lets my daughter or a daughter-in-law, both of whom are crusty and tough, know exactly what the rational woman wishes. And should my good sense go glimmering the way my mother's did, should I become a different, querulous person, incapable of comprehension, it should be less burdensome for them to make the necessary decisions because, in a shining, undemented moment, I have told them clearly what to do.

A DPA with another focus is also available. The Will to Live (a provocative metamorphosis of the phrase "living will") has been devised by the National Right to Life Committee, headquartered in Washington, D.C. The NRLC, founded in 1973 as a pro-life organization in response to the U.S. Supreme Court's *Roe vs. Wade* decision to legalize abortion—choice at the beginning of life—has since expanded its purview to battle choice at the end of life, in particular, euthanasia and a living will that allows you to specify the treatments that you do not want. Euthanasia in the NRLC's view includes not only assisted suicide but also withdrawal of life-support. The NRLC's Will to Live is adapted to the specific legal requirements of each of the fifty states. In every case, it follows the state's general form for a DPA and then, in a section called "General Presumption for Life," instructs your agent in great detail to maintain your life as long as possible. That section comprises eleven directives. The first three are these:

✦ I direct my health care provider(s) and health
care agent(s) to make health care decisions consistent with my general desire for the use of medical
treatment that would preserve my life, as well as for
the use of medical treatment that can cure, improve,
or reduce or prevent deterioration in any physical
or mental condition.

✦ Food and water are not medical treatment but
basic necessities. I direct my health care provider(s)
and health care agent(s) to provide me with food
and fluids orally, intravenously, by tube, or by
other means to the full extent necessary both
to preserve my life and to assure me the optimal
health possible.

✦ I direct that medication to alleviate my pain be
provided, as long as the medication is not used in
order to cause my death.

Other provisions direct administration of medication, CPR, and
every imaginable other medical procedure that might "correct, reverse, or alleviate life-threatening or health-impairing conditions,
or complications arising from those conditions." The document
also directs the agent to reject treatments or tissues obtained from
aborted fetuses. Then, it binds the agent to follow the directives
of the DPA even if the patient attempts suicide after the document
is signed. Nor is the quality of life forgotten: "I request and direct
that medical treatment and care be provided to me to preserve my
life without discrimination based on my age or physical or mental
disability or the 'quality' of my life." In addition, the Will to Live
form gives you room to specify what medications and treatments

may be withheld—or must be administered—in case of terminal illness or imminent death.

Though all Will to Live forms contain an identical "General Presumption for Life," some provide other stipulations. Georgia and Kansas, for two, allow you to designate a guardian for yourself, should the need arise. Other states bring in the matter of religious belief. Among them are Illinois, New Hampshire, and Virginia, which refer to this matter before listing the General Presumption for Life provisions. New Hampshire instructs the person executing a durable health care power of attorney that "If for moral or religious reasons you do not wish to be treated by a doctor or examined by a doctor for the certification that you lack capacity, you must say so in the document and name a person to be able to certify your lack of capacity. That person may not be your agent or alternate agent or any person ineligible to be your agent." Ineligible persons include caregivers, such as nursing home personnel. I find this instruction scary: Who better than people in the medical profession to certify incompetence? The Virginia version is even scarier: "My agent shall not authorize a course of treatment which he or she knows, or upon reasonable inquiry ought to know, is contrary to my religious beliefs or my basic values, whether expressed orally or in writing." *Ought to know*—the words stipulate a terrifying omniscience on the agent's part.

A friendlier, less in-your-face document, Five Wishes, which may be crafted to suit any temperament, is offered by an organization called Aging with Dignity. It consists of a DPA, a living will, and medical directives first on how comfortable you wish to be, then on how you wish to be treated in order to maintain your dignity. The fifth segment "gives you a chance to tell others how you want to be remembered and express other things that might be in your heart, like forgiveness." It is legal in thirty-five of the fifty states. Even in the holdouts, like Texas, Oregon, and New Hampshire, it may be accepted as a valid expression of your wishes.

A do-not-resuscitate order has a far narrower purpose than a DPA. It requests that cardiopulmonary resuscitation not be given if your heart or breathing should stop. In other words, it says that you should be allowed to die, not be shocked back into life, if you're on the final threshold or, as happens too often, have already crossed it. It also comes in two forms, one for an in-patient, the other for someone still at home. People with at-home DNRs are also provided with a plastic bracelet that holds a condensed version of the order. But if no DNR directive exists, or if it can't be found, medical personnel, from emergency squad technicians to hospital nurses, will exert superhuman efforts—defibrillators, oxygen, rib-cracking CPR—to pull the Lazarus-trick on a dying person or someone who is newly dead. Yes, the dead can sometimes, rudely, be brought back to life, even though the result is life in a persistent vegetative state. DNR orders can be obtained in every state, although each state honors only those DNRs that have been issued within its jurisdiction. The laws authorizing them, however, are not uniform but rather variations on a theme, subject to legislative preferences and quirks. Florida, for example, requires a diagnosis of terminal illness by two physicians before a DNR can be issued. As of January 1, 2000, Massachusetts has stipulated that a patient must be wearing a bracelet with the pertinent information before rescue squad workers and first responders are allowed to honor a DNR. So, even if you have such an order, you are not exempt from heroic measures, costs be damned, to save your life. (Where lies the heroism in cracking ancient ribs? I do not know.)

In some states, including Virginia during my mother's lifetime, a DNR is finite. It expires after the passage of a legislatively stipulated period of time and, starting from scratch, must be renewed. Anyone oriented toward life—and that means most of us, from caregiving professionals to family, friends, and neighbors—are aware that someone who says he doesn't want to be hauled back from the brink may very well change his mind. Health may improve, or terror may set in as death looms closer. After her first stroke, we saw my mother change her mind about entering Sunnyside. It was classic denial, it was magical thinking, as if destroying her application would also destroy any need to move into the Sunnyside community.

Timor mortis—people don't want to think about DNR orders. To do so is to admit death's stygian existence. Death, however, is a part of life. To see it as the invincible adversary, the avatar of endless night, constitutes an act of denial. But issues will rear themselves willy-nilly like untamable beasts. Better to bring them into the open and look at them in the light of day. Then they may be approached with logic rather than with the kind of heart-thumping panic that erases reason.

It's the good intentions of emergency medical technicians, their goal of defeating public enemy number one, that I wish to keep at bay. So, I go hunting for a DNR form. The venue is a trackless wilderness. It seems logical to start with the local rescue squad. They give me the impression that they do not know what I'm talking about and refer me to the agency in Richmond, the state capital, that oversees the operations of rescue squads throughout the Commonwealth. The agency bounces me back to the local establishment. Hostility colors the voices of the two people with whom I manage to talk. The subliminal content of what they tell me is that their role is to save lives, not pander to death. It is as if I am guilty of opting for unceasing darkness over light. What to do? I put in a call to Dr. Douglas, my mother's physician, who returns it three days later. His response? He doesn't know how I should go about getting the form. I think that indeed he knows but doesn't want to be bothered. (To be fair, I learn later that ignorance is widespread. Neither my own primary-care physician nor a private agency that sends non-medical caregivers into clients' homes knows how to go about getting a DNR form. But by then, I have the information and am glad to be able to tell them.) Time passes; other tasks, other interests beckon. But I see my mother slipping slowly but irremediably downhill. She needs saving from the saviors. For, extraordinary efforts to keep her from turning into a rainbow would not diminish her suffering but rather add to it.

Six months after the beginning of the search, the source of an out-of-hospital DNR form is at last discovered. A nurse, making the regular monthly visit to change my mother's catheter, tells me that the form is available at the usual source everywhere; the office of her home health-care agency. Ours is located just around the corner in a small shopping enclave, not grand enough to be called a plaza or a mall. How simple! Instanter, I hie myself down there. The form is produced without delay, without any indication that I'm doing something bothersome or, at worst, unthinkable. It is a one-page, two-sided document printed on yellow paper. The front side, on which the patient's name and the date are filled in, features two paragraphs, one declaring that the person requesting the DNR understands its import and the other stating the contrary. A doctor is to check the paragraph that applies. The reverse side bears lines for the doctor's John Hancock and that of the person to whom the DNR pertains. At the bottom of the page, a strip of paper with the pertinent details may be detached for insertion into the clear plastic bracelet.

I take the form to Dr. Douglas's office and pick it up the next day. He has signed and dated the order. He has also checked the paragraph stating that Sarah does indeed understand it. In theory, all that's needed now is her signature. But she does not understand (he knows that!). Furthermore, she can no longer write. So, I sign her name and add my own, followed by the letters POA, in parentheses; the letters refer to the business power of attorney that she did give me. The act lies in a shady area: She long ago signed a living will that designated me as decision-maker, but because she has given no health-care power of attorney, no one is legally her agent. But I hope, should the order be questioned, that the provisions in her living will may be enough to indicate her wishes.

How odd it is that our lives may depend on bits of paper. How chilling, that we do not—cannot—trust one another, that touch and speech do not suffice.

The original order is affixed with magnets to the front of the refrigerator. Copies are made—one for the doctor, one for my files. Rosa fills the plastic bracelet with the strip detached from the DNR and buckles it around my mother's wrist. My mother picks at it. She makes a face and says, "Ugh! No, no!" Thirty seconds after it was put on, the bracelet is taken off. I do not see it again. I harbor a not unreasonable suspicion that her caregivers may ignore the DNR posted on the refrigerator if there's an emergency, for they have a vested interest in her survival. She is their livelihood.

This is the first DNR. It will be renewed three times. Later, the Commonwealth of Virginia will change the rules, authorizing a Durable DNR order, so that the first DNR is also the last, unless it is specifically revoked.

Chasing Death Down

... the way death happens slow sometimes. How
sometimes people are dead before their hearts stop
beating. How sometimes they walk around that
way for a long time before their bodies let them go.
Sometimes they even have to chase death down.

—Sheri Reynolds, *A Gracious Plenty*

TWO YEARS AFTER the second stroke, Sarah still smiles much and seems contented for the most part, though sometimes she cries or fails to recognize familiar faces. At this point, her vocabulary is limited mainly to "Good," "Yes," and the names of family and friends, although in case of dire need she can summon strong language, language the likes of which she'd never used before the strokes. The damaged brain releases a thesaurus that the intact brain had locked away. Shortly after she recovered from the two months of terror induced by hearing Dr. Douglas talk casually about a mastectomy, I come to see her, and the caregiver on duty mentions that it's time to make an appointment for a checkup with Dr. D. Sarah perks up at that, scowls, and says without any trouble at all, "Dougie, Dougie, damn Dougie, go to hell." That is my signal to find her another primary-care physician. She never again sees Dr. D. He is splendidly replaced by James LaGrua, a young osteopath in his mid-thirties. His hair is dark and fine, his eyes an astonishing warm golden brown, and his generous smile reaches from ear to ear. According her every courtesy, he speaks to her directly, rather than sideways, as if she weren't present, to the person who has accompanied her. From the first, it is apparent that she does not fear him.

It's not easy to visit with someone who cannot hold a conversation. My own tactic is to read to her. Every afternoon at four, just after she awakes from her nap and has been wheeled from bed to toilet to motorized recliner by her caregiver, I sit on the hassock directly opposite the recliner and open the book of the moment. The stories range from *The Wonderful Wizard of Oz* and Rudyard Kipling's *Just So Stories* to both chronicles recounting the adventures of Winnie the Pooh. One chapter at a time, the tales wrap themselves around the afternoon with the cozy comfort of a quilt. And Sarah, who still has some of her wits about her, if not her speech, signals understanding with motions of her hands. She shakes with laughter at the impertinent questions asked by the elephant's child before he set off to the great, grey-green, greasy Limpopo River to get his nose (and the noses of all elephants thereafter) stretched by the crocodile. She pantomimes Pooh trying to tug off the honey jar into which he'd stuck his head. The readings become so much a given in Sarah's afternoons that when she hears the soft swish of the front door opening and the snick of the latch as it closes, she discovers sounds of her own to greet my entrance. At first, they are the crowing squeals of a happy baby. But in a matter of days they transform themselves into one loud, clear, peremptory word: "Story!"

My siblings find their own devices for countering aphasia. My brothers substitute motion for talk. Each according to his fashion takes her for rides. In clement weather, Joe, a grizzled and thoughtful graphic artist two years younger than I, comes daily to walk her little white dog, Muffin, and on warm days pushes our mother around the neighborhood in her wheelchair. Bob, a businessman my junior by seven years, lifts her into his car and chauffeurs Sarah on drives down the country roads that she's always loved. His wife, sitting in the back seat, chatters endlessly and feeds her cookies. The elder of my two sisters, Sarah Jane, born when I was a sophomore in high school (and mortified at having to suffer a pregnant mother through half of the school year) uses things in lieu of conversation. After flying down from her home in Massachusetts just before Christmas, she goes shopping for new decorations for house and tree; she celebrates other special occasions, like our mother's birthday and the Fourth of July, with a tank of tropical fish, a video of fireworks, a catered feast. Each new thing provokes Sarah Jane into filling silence with detailed commentary on its benefits and beauties. And Ginny, the sister born the week that I left for college, specializes in touch. When she comes in from Texas every three months or so, she gets to work right away, trimming Sarah's new pixie haircut or manicuring her nails, painting them mauve, pink, silver, and, once, an iridescent green. Our mother relaxes and smiles—our mother, the woman who, until her second stroke and the scalp-shaving operation to relieve the pressure on her brain, had sported frizzy beauty parlor curls and plain nails because she had no idle minutes to invest in anything beyond a basically neat appearance. "Good," she invariably says to Ginny's ministrations. "Yes," she says to fish and rides and stories.

Everyone who comes to visit regularly devises some useful tactic for dealing with my mother's speechlessness. The minister of her church kneels, prays for twenty droning minutes, rises, and leaves. A first cousin, tiny, seventy-odd, and ditsy, always delivers a stand-up series of mainly naughty one-liners. She giggles, and Sarah giggles back with fine exuberance (although I can never decide whether my mother's laughter is triggered by the jokes or simply by the cousin herself). Friends discover something that might be called the strength-in-numbers strategy: two people who are able to talk entertaining one who can't. And they use reminiscence to tap into Sarah's long-term memory. Tell her that it is Tuesday or tell her that the sky is falling, she will not remember a thing five minutes later. But talk about the past—about World War II when her first set of children was young and her husband had gone to England as a soldier, about the years that she had cared for her own mother, about serving on the town council and planting gardens for a civic beautification project, Sarah responds with one of her all-purpose words or by painting pictures on the air.

That's a tactic that I can use, too—reminiscence. One result of sorting through the cardboard cartons stored in the basement is five photo albums, starting with pictures of ancestors, then moving chronologically through Sarah's childhood, early married life. motherhood, World War II, and on to her later years and their accomplishments. The last album contains snapshots made of her after the second stroke, with her new pixie haircut and the big faux-gold ten-cent-store earrings brought by the ditsy cousin. As I complete the albums, I take them over. She is most intrigued by the album with photos of 1930, when she and my father, newly wed, had driven across the country to attend Stanford University. Many photos show their trusty Model A Ford, and many, labeled on the back by my father, variously portray my mother. In one, she stands by a doorway at "one of the better auto camps in Arizona"; in another she climbs, dressed in skirt and stockings, up a ladder to an Anasazi cliff dwelling in Montezuma

Castle National Monument; in several, she sits on the steps of the cottage they rented in Palo Alto. As I turn the pages and read my father's captions, transferred to typed labels, she looks intently at the photos. "Yes. Good." And sometimes she manages my father's name: "Joe."

One morning, no-nonsense Rosa, the LPN who tends Sarah during the third shift and flushes out impacted feces as necessary, takes me aside and says quite sternly, "Don't you be upsetting your mother, you hear. You been talking about your father. And there goes Miss Sarah, all night tossing and turning and calling out, 'Joe, Joe, Joe.' Now she don't need that."

After twenty-six years of widowhood, twenty-six years of freedom, can she really be missing him? "This is new," I say.

"Not just him," Rosa replies. "People who have passed on—her mama and her sister, too, though they don't upset her, they light up her eyes. She don't say much, but she say their names. Lately, middle of the night, she been visiting right much with the dead. Old people do that."

Now that the phenomenon has been pointed out to me, I notice that she visits the dead in the daytime, too. I go to see her, book in hand for our story, but she's not in the present moment. "Jannette, Jannette," she calls softly. Her hand makes a beckoning motion. It's not I to whom she refers. She's calling her mother. She also calls out and beckons to living people, who are not there, especially her youngest child, Ginny. One day, as the fourth year after the second stroke approaches, I'm told that she spent the night calling my younger daughter, Hannah. The hair rises on the back of my neck. It's Hannah's thirty-sixth birthday—or would have been. Hannah is dead. She died in 1995 of a breast cancer that metastasized to her bones. And I helped her die. My elder daughter, Lisa, and I decided to pull the plug.

PULLING THE PLUG—removing life-support paraphernalia in all its guises, feeding tube, catheter, intravenous drip, respirator— is a controversial concept. It first came to full, roaring public attention with the case of Karen Ann Quinlan, a New Jersey girl who collapsed at a party on April 15, 1975, when she was twenty-one years old. At the time, campaigning against the use of illegal substances—and leaping to conclusions, newspapers reported that she had been felled by drugs and alcohol. But evidence points to another cause: a combination of two things that do not mix—alcohol and the legal drug Darvon, which she took to ease menstrual pain. She ceased breathing twice that night, with each spell of breathlessness lasting about 15 minutes. That amounts to nearly half an hour in which her brain was starved of oxygen. After being taken to a hospital, she lapsed into a coma. In subsequent days, her condition worsened, and all of the doctors who examined her declared that the damage she had suffered could not be reversed and that she had entered a persistent vegetative state without any possibility for recovery.

A persistent vegetative state, as defined by the doctors who introduced the term in 1972, is one in which the condition of a patient has reached a state of "wakefulness without awareness." These comatose people have no cerebral cortical function; they are unconscious and unaware but do have sleep-wake cycles with full or partial brain-stem autonomic functions. The condition is further described this way:

> Patients in a persistent vegetative state may be
> aroused by certain stimuli, opening their eyes if
> they are closed, changing their facial expressions,
> or even moving their limbs. Furthermore, they can
> grind their teeth, swallow, smile, shed tears, grunt,

moan, or scream without any reason. Their heads
and eyes can follow a moving object or move
toward a loud sound. Yet, these responses have
been observed in patients in whom careful study
has shown no evidence of awareness. Consistent
with a persistent vegetative state is a lack of sustained visual pursuit. Although they may move
their eyes, patients in a vegetative state neither
fixate on a visual object nor track a moving target
with their eyes. . . . Although these patients may
exhibit behavior that appears to be the result of
conscious thought and reasoning, these behaviors
are merely reflexive and do not indicate awareness.

These behaviors also engender hope in the parents, spouses,
children, and friends who stand by watching. The absence of
awareness may be impossible to understand. And it must have
been that Karen Ann's family felt that, despite the odds, she would
wake again. At that point her life was sustained by a respirator to
assure regular breathing and a feeding tube, implanted in her
stomach, to deliver nutrients and water ("nutrition" and "hydration" are the impersonal technical terms). The debate, loud and
furious, began when her parents, abandoning hope, sought to
disconnect her but ran into a hair-splitting distinction about
whether "extraordinary means" had been brought into play to
keep her alive, although even minimal recovery could not be expected. She would never again wake to care for herself in any way.
The primary-care physician deemed the respirator to be indeed an
extraordinary means but not the feeding tube. By then the Quinlans had gone to court in an attempt to withdraw life support. In
1976, the case went all the way to the New Jersey Supreme Court,

which honored the Quinlans' request. But the decision was moot, for the respirator had been withdrawn, and Karen was breathing successfully on her own. She did not, therefore, fit the standard definitions of brain-death. The ironic outcome: feeding tube still in place, she lived in a nursing home for nearly eight more years until pneumonia finally claimed her.

It's worth mentioning the four legal precedents that were set in the New Jersey Supreme Court's decision on the Quinlan case. First, a patient has the right to refuse treatment even if doing so may lead to death. Second, if a patient is mentally incompetent, someone else may make decisions for them. Third, a decision that might lead to the death of a mentally incompetent person is best made not by the courts but by families, in consultation with their physicians. Last, any decision about end-of-life care should consider burdens and benefits: the treatment's degree of harshness and the patient's chance for recovery. These points are still not widely accepted by people of all persuasions—politicians, for one, and clergy, and even the judiciary.

Another controversy as hotly contested as that of Karen Ann Quinlan centered on Nancy Beth Cruzan, a twenty-five-year-old Missourian involved in an automobile accident in early 1983. The rescue squad paramedics who rescued her and restored her breathing estimated that her brain had lacked oxygen for 15 to 20 minutes before they arrived. Like Karen Ann Quinlan, she had suffered irreversible brain damage and was diagnosed as being in a permanent vegetative state. The doctors, however, told her family that, although she would never wake, never return to her old self, she could nonetheless be kept alive indefinitely with food and water delivered through a surgically implanted feeding tube. For five years, at a cost well over half a million dollars, she was kept alive in this fashion. During this time her condition deteriorated drastically. She had become quadriplegic, her legs and arms had contracted, she responded only reflexively to sound and perhaps pain. Before the accident, she had told a housemate that she would not want to live if sickness or injury meant that she had no chance of returning to a state that was "at least halfway normal." Her parents asked the court in Jaspar County, Missouri, to be allowed to terminate hydration and nutrition. The request was judicially granted in early 1988. The state immediately filed an appeal. Would removing the tube be in accord with Nancy's wishes or would it amount to criminal homicide? In November, 1988, the Missouri Supreme Court denied Nancy's parents the right to make decisions on her behalf. The Court's position reflected its view that the inherent sanctity of life (even insensate life) took precedence over any quality-of-life issues. The family appealed this decision to the U.S. Supreme Court, which, in June, 1990, came down on the side of the right to die but ducked the issue at hand. Arguing that states could set "reasonable" limits on the exercise of that right, it sent the case back to the state of Missouri. The Cruzans went back to the Jaspar County Court, where some of Nancy's friends testified about her expressed wishes. The judge decided that there was enough evidence that Nancy would not have wanted to live given her hopeless condition. And Nancy's physician became convinced that withdrawal of treatment would be proper. The tube was removed on December 15. Nancy died eleven days later.

More than ten years have passed since then. There's still no end to the conflict between individual wishes and state authority. Is the removal of life-sustaining tubes and respirators from irreversibly comatose patients a criminal act or a merciful deliverance? The public stance has often been that it is not the patient's condition that would cause death but rather the removal of food and water, the provision of which has been considered basic care, not medical treatment. In other words, removal would amount to euthanasia. No, that's a euphemism. It would amount to murder. I cannot help but wonder, however, if the people who vociferously advocate continuation of life support for people languishing in a persistent vegetative state would choose such maintenance for themselves—consciousness and costs be damned.

I think of the case of Hugh Finn, a television anchorman who suffered a ruptured aorta in an automobile accident in 1995. His brain, like those of Karen Ann Quinlan and Nancy Cruzan, had been starved of oxygen long enough to put him into a persistent vegetative state. And like the young women, he was kept alive by feeding-tube administration of nutrients and water. After more than three years of watching her husband being kept alive but not living, Michelle Finn wanted to remove his feeding tube. He had drafted a statement to the effect that he did not want life-sustaining measures in such a situation but had not signed it. The Virginia Supreme Court supported Michelle's position, saying that withdrawal of food and water from a permanently comatose patient simply allowed the patient to die naturally, but Hugh Finn's parents and brothers made strenuous objection. At that point, the Commonwealth of Virginia, in the person of its governor, James S. Gilmore, III, weighed in, claiming that removal of the tube was tantamount to homicide. The Supreme Court, however, rejected Gilmore's case. The tube was removed, and Hugh Finn died eight days later. Virginia eventually paid Michelle Finn $48,000 to cover the expenses that she had incurred to battle the Commonwealth for the right to let her husband die in peace. And all this happened more than twenty years after Karen Ann Quinlan's ordeal, and eight years after the Supreme Court's right-to-die decision in the case of Nancy Cruzan.

These three cases all feature well-known people—well-known because of intense media interest in their cases or, with Hugh Finn, because of his prominence on television. But the three merely represent thousands upon thousands of cases that receive little or no publicity.

Tina Cartrette exemplifies the legion of the anonymous, although her case figured briefly in North Carolina newspapers. She had been disabled throughout her life by cerebral palsy, mental retardation, and frequent seizures. Her mother, who had made decisions for Tina during her entire life, served as her legal guardian. When Tina was 29, she was hospitalized for recurring infections, high fevers, and seizures. She could have left the hospital after life-support mechanisms, the expectable tubes and a respirator, were attached, but no skilled-care facility had room for her. In November, 2000, her mother decided to let her die. She acted in keeping with doctors' opinions that doing so would not amount to neglect. Food, water, and antibiotics were withdrawn; the respirator was turned off. As it happened, Tina could breathe on her own. Then the state leaped in. The Governor's Advocacy Council for the Disabled went to court and obtained an order that not only transferred guardianship to someone else but caused reinstatement of tube-feeding and hydration. It was not a judge who issued the order, but rather an assistant clerk of court, a man of no medical standing and a stranger to the case. In March, 2001, Tina's mother sued for reinstatement as her guardian and succeeded. There ended the first brief account that I read. The second caught my attention at the beginning of September, 2001. The headline read, "Disabled woman caught in guardianship battle dies." For the two preceding months, she had been curled in a fetal position, with her fists closed so tightly that her fingernails sometimes grew into her palms. This contorted posture is typical

in someone kept alive for a long time by means of artificial nutrition and hydration; Karen Ann Quinlan and Nancy Cruzan were
also folded in on themselves. Tina died only a few days after being
taken off life-support for a second time. The Governor's Advocacy
Council for the Disabled issued a statement that chills me. The
newspaper put it this way: "The news of Cartrette's death was a
disappointment to advocates for the disabled." It goes on to quote
the Council's executive director as saying, "We're glad that we
intervened. I think we brought attention to the issue. We don't
want people deciding that our lives have less value."

The profound issue here is the sanctity of life versus the quality of life. A divine abstraction is pitted against an earthbound
reality. I am immensely grateful that no one interfered when Lisa
and I made the decision to withdraw Hannah's life support. I'm
sure that such decisions are made and such actions are taken
quietly every day. No advocates, no governors, no reporters to stir
public attention. Instead, family and physicians act in gentle concert on behalf of the irretrievably comatose patient.

Who was Hannah, my third child and younger daughter? She
was tall and willow-slender with waist-length dark hair. She was
a single mother whose marriage had lasted no longer than a flash
of firefly light. After high school, she took a year off to decide
what might best come next. Next turned out to be the pursuit of
an undergraduate degree in biology, but studies were interrupted
after the first year because of her CB radio. En route from school
to home (with much dirty laundry in tow), she began talking with
big-rig truck drivers, then started riding with them. Some let her
drive. Within months she had her own trucker's license but
needed driver's education for tractor-trailers. A trucking firm in
South Dakota ran a school to train its own drivers. She applied and
was accepted. For the next two years, she drove a tractor-trailer,

starting with a trip from the Midwest to the state of Washington. On that maiden voyage in 1980, her first call home expressed dismay, for Mount St. Helens had erupted, and wind-borne ash had stopped all big-rig traffic to the state. She was stuck in Montana. But education beckoned, and she became a full-time student for most of the rest of her life, earning an undergraduate degree and a master's in biology. Truck-driving paid for the works. When cancer first struck, she was 27, a doctoral student at North Carolina State University. After a mastectomy, she was cancer-free for about six years. Then, as she was just getting under way with a new doctoral program at the University of Virginia, she began feeling unwell. Like a silent marauder, the cancer had metastasized, going to her bones. Despite its new location, it could be identified as breast cancer by the character of its cells. She undertook massive sessions of chemotherapy—and somehow, miraculously, she did not lose much of her long, straight brown hair. But she was unable to go to school, unable to work, and subsisted on Social Security disability payments in a low-income housing project, where she lived with a longtime male companion. Her thirteen-year-old daughter visited but resided with her father, Hannah's one-time husband. One evening, for reasons that we shall never know, she had a seizure. Her companion called the rescue squad, but by the time they arrived, she had not breathed for nearly ten minutes. Nonetheless, they shocked the breath back into her before transporting her to the hospital at the University of Virginia. Early the next morning, her companion's mother called me in North Carolina, where my husband, the Chief, and I were staying in our spring and summer home, to say that Hannah was in the hospital and unconscious, that the prognosis was not hopeful. After a frantic day of making ready to move back to Virginia, I traveled north, arriving at the hospital just moments before Lisa came in from Wisconsin. We saw Hannah lying in bed, her eyes closed, her breathing steady. Since she had come to the hospital, she had not waked. Nutrients and water were being delivered by a tube, and yellow urine dribbled into the Foley catheter bag attached to the side of her bed. A young female doctor-in-residence took us aside then to tell us details of Hannah's condition and give us options for her treatment. "She's in a persistent vegetative state," the doctor said and explained that Hannah had sustained irreversible damage when her brain was deprived of oxygen after the seizure. But we had choices. We could keep her attached to life support, keep her alive, although she would never recover consciousness, or we could remove life support. The doctor delivered the news in a matter-of-fact manner, but her voice contained an infinite sadness and gentleness. Lisa and I did not need to discuss the situation. It would be agonizing for us to keep her alive, and we asked immediately that the tubes be detached. And so they were, mere moments after we left.

My two sons arrived the next day, one from his out-of-town construction job, the other with his wife from Illinois. We visited Hannah daily and talked to her, hoping that she'd somehow recognize that we were there. Lisa brushed her sister's long hair. The one person who was not there was Hannah's daughter, who had been forbidden by her father and stepmother to make the trip with us; their reason was that the child was too young and tender to look upon her dying mother. On the second day after the tubes had been removed, Hannah seemed agitated. Her mouth moved, her eyelids fluttered. Sometimes she seemed to be looking out into the room. That evening, her companion called us to say that she was regaining consciousness. A forlorn hope, but one that we understood completely, for it is the hope experienced by many other families with someone in an irreversible coma. Not one of us wanted her to die. Yet, not one of us, for all the wishing in the world, could bring her back to life. She was alive, yes, but not living. We'd go home for supper and weep. On the fourth day, September 18, 1995, she died. She was thirty-five years old. According to her wishes, she was cremated and her ashes scattered on the summit of Reddish Knob, the second highest mountain in Virginia. The day shone bright and cool on the cusp of autumn. In rattletraps and Lincoln Town Cars, on Harley Davidson motorcycles, her family and friends made the journey and assembled on the mountaintop. Her companion gave me an immense bunch of wildflowers—goldenrod, purple asters, dogwood leaves that oncoming fall had touched with scarlet. People read poems or made memorial remarks. The companion scattered her ashes, I tossed the flowers over them, and we made our ways home. Sorrow—heart-rending, soul-shaking sorrow—but what else could we have done? It has been truly said that sorrow rusts the soul. Best, we thought, to let her go peacefully, for doing so would help heal that sorrow and lift us out of the depths and let us move forward with our own lives so long as they should last. And she would no longer be in the wasteland between life and death. There would be an ending, and endings signal new beginnings. In no way have we ever regretted letting her go. The enduring sadness lies in having had to make that choice.

Hannah, Karen Ann Quinlan, Nancy Cruzan, Hugh Finn, Tina Cartrette—though unconscious, all of them could have been kept alive until age or illness gave them release, but to what purpose? Is it more merciful to sustain insentient flesh, to keep it unnaturally alive, than to let it go? Wesley J. Smith, author of *Culture of Death,* sees the situation this way: "Withholding sustenance from an aged or disabled person in order to *cause* death is simply wrong, because it is based not on the patient's actual medical needs, but rather on the perceived moral worth of a human life." He speaks from a life-at-all-costs point of view and damns the term "persistent vegetative state," saying that it is "a medical diagnosis involving violence of logic and language (human being = vegetable)." He also writes, "Not too many years ago, it was considered unethical, indeed potentially a criminal act, to stop feeding and hydrating an incompetent patient." His opinions are at best wrongheaded. The word *vegetative* applied to a condition in no way equates human being and vegetable but rather refers to an extreme slowing down of involuntary bodily functions. As for the ethics and criminality of withdrawing life support, it might be well to remember that not long ago, certainly within my lifetime, delivering food and water by intubation was completely impossible. I think that a decision to retard death by continuing life support for people who can never wake is an act of cruelty that springs, like a trickster, from a profound, self-centered fear. Those who make such a decision do not really do so on behalf of someone loved but comatose; rather, they make it for themselves. It is a way of warding off their own mortality, of downright denying it, and all in the name of the sanctity of life. The other side of the coin is that in keeping alive a person who cannot wake, they retard the resolution of their grief.

To keep the dead and close-to-dying alive is something new in human history. It happened only an eye-blink of time ago. Until well into the twentieth century, most Americans died at home, for there were no medical interventions available to keep life going in extremis. Human beings and protohumans have walked upright on the earth for millennia. From *Sahelanthropus tchadensis*, whose six- to seven-million-year-old skull was discovered in the summer of 2001 in northern Chad, through the famous Lucy, who dates back some three million years, and on to the Neanderthals and

Homo sapiens, no one was snatched back once the grim reaper had put in a claim. This is not to say that there were no people well versed in mending wounds and administering healing potions; rather, no one could—or was expected to—resurrect the dying. It is only with the last century's exponential broadening of medical and technological knowledge that the widespread use of measures to save the sick and injured have come to the fore. At the turn of the century, 1899 to 1900, life expectancy in the United States was only forty-seven years. Granted, it has increased tremendously because of such things as improved nutrition, antibiotics, and vaccinations and inoculations against diseases like smallpox, diphtheria, whooping cough, and polio that not long ago carried off many people. Our water is clean now, thanks to treatment plants, and our streets clear of sewage. Hearts, kidneys, lungs, and livers may be transplanted, giving some recipients a bright new lease on longevity. Nowadays, instead of dying quickly of infectious disease, we have been given not only that lease on longevity but also the concomitant likelihood that we will suffer from drawn-out, chronic illnesses in our seventies and eighties. And we are often kept alive when we have ceased to find purpose in existence. But to all of us there comes a time to die, and better to die as peacefully and painlessly as possible. The Buddha has said it well: "Just as the strong current of a waterfall / Cannot be reversed, / So the movement of a human life / Is also irreversible."

Marilyn Webb, author of *The Good Death,* states the current dilemma cogently:

> Now that life can be almost mercilessly extended,
> we are finding that we have failed as a nation to
> assess adequately the goals of modern treatment—

when treatment makes sense, when it undermines
the well-being of both patient and family, and what
happens then. There is no cultural agreement about
when treatment should stop, and no good social
provisions for long-term care.

Release or hang on for dear life—what do thinkers more objective than I have to say? The plight of Hugh Finn, a Catholic,
brought considered response from his church. (Ironically, his career
as a newsman had included reportage on both the Quinlan and
Cruzan cases.) John J. Paris, a Jesuit and professor of bioethics at
Boston College, frames the fundamental question in an article on
Hugh Finn's "right to die": "Is there a moral obligation to continue
intravenous feeding of an irreversibly comatose patient?" Sur-
veying Catholic teaching on the subject, he finds that the Church
has clearly and repeatedly stated over the last 400 years that no
comatose person need be kept alive if there is no hope of regaining physical and mental functions. Father Paris quotes from a
statement made in 1990 by the Roman Catholic bishops of Texas,
who described patients in a persistent vegetative state as "human
beings stricken with a lethal pathology which, without artificial
nutrition and hydration, will lead to death." In the bishops' view,
withdrawing life support "is not abandoning the person. Rather,
it is accepting the fact that the person has come to the end of his
or her pilgrimage and should not be impeded from taking the final
step." Morality requires that the concerns of the spirit be placed
above the needs of the flesh. Thus, it is immoral to prolong the life
of a person who cannot return to awareness, who can no longer
strive to find meaning in being alive. This opinion is reinforced by
a statement made by Richard Doerflinger, assistant director for
policy development of the National Conference of Catholic Bishops.

He says "We all have an obligation to make reasonable efforts to preserve life and health, but no one is obliged to accept a treatment that would have more burdens than benefits. This includes pain, suffering, and expense, for patients as well as for families."

What does Jewish tradition have to say about these matters? I talk with Ariel Friedlander, rabbi of a Reform congregation. We meet in her study, an inviting room paneled with wood and lined with books. In her late thirties, dark-haired and comfortably plump, she speaks with a softly passionate voice. Though she is an American, it contains more than a hint of her upbringing in Britain. Using exegeses from the Torah and the Talmud, she presents views on bioethical matters such as assisted suicide and withdrawing life-support. The central issue is, Do new developments in medicine and technology come within the bounds of the Talmud—that is, the law? When does life begin? When does it end? She says, "The burden is on us to make these decisions. But Reform Judaism is not a religion without boundaries. The laws are there to make a fence around the Torah." I am provided, too, with suggestions for reading and a list of Responsa—scholarly answers from the Central Conference of American Rabbis—to thousands of questions about Reform Judaism and Jewish life. The topics range from abortion to zodiac (signs of the, on synagogue windows). As we talk, the computer prints out a response to questions on the treatment of the terminally ill. I ask her, too, about her understanding of the term "quality of life." "The thing I fear most is pain," she says, "and then the inability to take care of myself. Quality of life means being able to live a life in the world with what you consider the minimum requirements of being able to continue to be here—what you're physically and mentally able to do." The implication is that if body and mind shut down, quality is transformed from a positive characteristic into one that is negative: fullness turns into a vacuum. Only when I leave do I note that Ariel Friedlander has allotted me a generous hour and a half. There were no silences.

As soon as I'm home, I read the Central Conference of American Rabbis' response on the treatment of the terminally ill. It posits two cases, that of a baby with a progressive brain disease that may not kill her until her teens and that of a 95-year-old woman with Alzheimer's disease. What in each case is the best approach to medical treatment? As I read, a divine instruction from Deuteronomy comes to mind: "I have set before you life and death, blessing and cursing: therefore choose life, that both thou and thy seed may live." And this is the thrust of the response, that "If the doctrine of life's essential holiness means anything at all, it means that we must stand in reverence before the very fact of life, the gift of God that renders us human. And this reverence does not diminish as human strength declines, for the dying person still possesses life, a life stamped indelibly with the image of God until the moment of death." Thus, euthanasia and assisted suicide are out, for both are sinful, nor would either even be considered in the cases of the baby and the old woman. Human law may give such acts sanction under certain conditions, but God's law does not.

The cessation of medical treatment, however, is a different matter. Such action holds a problem, of course, that of distinguishing between an act of killing and the removal of an impediment to death. But the first may be understood as a willed event in which someone else actively hastens the moment of the patient's death, while the second may be viewed as eliminating an unnatural barrier to the natural process. The criterion for leaving the barrier in place or removing it is medical efficacy. If it is therapeutic and adds zest to the patient's quality of life, then it should stay in place. If not, if it simply prolongs the process of dying

without positive benefit, then it should go. And if there is a duty
to heal the sick, what should be done if the patient is beyond healing? The response states, "One is required to take action to save
life only when such action has a reasonable chance of success. . . .
One is under no obligation to take useless actions, actions which
clearly do not contribute to the rescue of another person." Measures that do not heal are not considered to be medicine, although
they may certainly, futilely, be administered. Healing, if it can be
done, is obligate; the use of measures that serve only to prolong
suffering is not. But does delivering food and water through feeding tubes constitute medical treatment? Only when nutrition and
hydration enhance the patient's life. Otherwise, life support of this
kind serves only to delay the inevitable.

"There comes a point in time," the response reads, "when all
the technologies, the chemicals, the surgeries, and the machines
which comprise the lifesaving arsenal of modern medicine,
become counterproductive, a point when all that medical science
can effectively do for a patient is to infinitely delay his inevitable
death." This passage, which pushes me back willy-nilly to my
younger daughter's final days, brings tears. It hurts to recognize
this moment.

What of the baby and the old woman? The response advises
that the baby be given comfort care as long as she may live and
that her death not be delayed by artificial means. As for the
grande dame, the response's view is that Alzheimer's disease is
surely killing her and that random, opportunistic infections need
not be treated with antibiotics, which would serve only as "pointless hindrances to her death." The response concludes that "the
removal of an impediment is not an act of killing at all, not even
passive killing, but in fact a corrective measure taken against a situation which we have wrongly allowed to occur. For while Jewish

tradition forbids us to kill a terminal patient, it also forbids us to delay her death unnecessarily." Each patient, however, is unique; each family must weigh the options. No hard and fast rule determines whether to support life or let it go.

Moderate Protestant opinion would agree. I meet with John Peterson, the minister of a local Presbyterian church. We sit in his comfortable office, I in an armchair, he in a hand-crafted rocker that he tells me was made of hickory and oak by the Amish in New Wilmington, Pennsylvania. Sunlight streaming through a picture window illuminates the beige walls, on one of which hangs a large oil painting of a rugged mountain rendered in steely blues and greens beneath an ice-blue sky. Shelves, made of warm brown wood and packed with books, line another wall. An attorney for eight years before he was ordained, John Peterson is doubly qualified to discuss bioethical issues. Faith permeates his opinions. "Life is God's gift to us," he says. "We hold it sacred as a gift from God. And part of life is death. We need not fear death, for we have the promise of God's continuing care."

At the beginning of our conversation, he makes clear the Presbyterian stance on suicide—"Taking death into one's own hands is usurping the authority of God." And on assisted suicide: the church is not supportive but recognizes that there is an individual right to say yea or nay to care. As with Reform Judaism, professional or private acts on the part of someone else that are designed to speed a patient's death cannot be countenanced, but the patient may voluntarily elect to forego treatment. To do so presupposes an ability to make such decisions. As for life support, if it is used as a means for healing, it is well and good, but if it is used solely to keep someone alive when there is no hope for healing, it is, at best, misguided. John Peterson says, "The quality of life at the end is more important than the quantity. It is a gift not to perpetuate the suffering." Thus, natural barriers to a natural process may be removed without guilt or recrimination.

One case, however, poses what he considers the ultimate ethical dilemma. What is the best course for someone who has had a pacemaker installed and then develops an illness that debilitates and eventually kills? The pacemaker keeps the person alive. Without it, death would quickly ensue. But is it like life support? Even if the patient so wishes, can a doctor ethically remove it? John Peterson has found no answer.

Rocking gently in his handmade chair, he speaks, too, of the fear of death and dying that pervade our culture. "In Scotland," he tells me, "they put you in a rough wooden box and put you in the ground. None of this business of chemicals and coffin that will preserve you for two hundred years. With the funeral home industry, we seem to deny the natural cycle." His own mother was buried in a churchyard with a tree on her grave. He says, "It's important to have a touch-point, a place you can go to and remember that person."

Touch-point—an apt and lovely way to describe a stimulus for memory! And the phrase radiates optimism. John Peterson gives an illustration, the best one he's experienced, of a family handling the end of life. As an aunt lay terminally ill in a hospital, her family gathered in her room to share stories and laughter, and she was very much part of this lively event. It was not a death watch that brought everyone together, no. It was instead a profound and vital impulse to celebrate her life. He says, "They all approached death not with fear and trembling but with affirmation and hope."

Before I leave, I ask about the painting of the mountain, which looks as if it might portray an ice-bound peak in the Rockies. John rises and takes it from the wall. It bears a legend on the back:

"Watzman, July 1974." This particular mountain rises magnificent in the Austrian Alps.

And how does a religion not in the Judeo-Christian tradition regard the business of chasing death down by assisted suicide or removal of life support? I look to Islam for answers, only to find that Islamic views on these matters are not always easy to come by. Once the Mid-East, where Islam arose, was the world's leader in scientific thinking and discoveries, and this at a time in which the West was still caught in the toils of the Middle Ages, with its emphasis on salvation and crusades to spread the faith. But in the Arab world, medicine and mathematics were premier foci of attention. Indeed, Arab scientists came across the useful concept of zero, and algebra—the word itself is Arabic—sprang into being through their studies. And, eyes on the heavens, they made noteworthy progress in the study of astronomy; many of the names used today for the stars of the first magnitude come from the Arabic, and, amid a roster that is predominantly Greek, they shine like jewels—Betelgeuse, Aldebaran, Rigel, Deneb, Vega, and a host of others. But as the West emerged from a world governed by theology and embarked on grand adventures such as the Renaissance, the Enlightenment, and space flight, the people of the Mid-East and those in Europe and Asia who had been brought under the aegis of Islam entered a period of stasis, of falling behind. The reasons are many and complex, among them centuries of war and a deep economic divide between the few rich and the mass of the poor. A perception sprang into being that the Qur'an was the one source of truth and that Westerners were infidels. Western science, seemingly godless, therefore became suspect. So, I look for a Muslim, who is not only a devout person but also a scholar well-versed in bioethical issues. Dr. Abdulaziz Sachedina, professor of Islamic Studies in the Department of Religious

Studies at the University of Virginia, fits the bill. He has written widely on bioethics, including papers on such matters as "Problems in Defining Brain Death in Islamic Jurisprudence" and " 'Right to Die?': Muslim Views About End of Life Decisions."

We meet in his office, which is situated in a red-brick building deep in the closely packed labyrinth of the university's campus. Luckily, I have a friend who guides me there. Dr. Sachedina opens the door and smiles. He is a slender sixty-year-old man of medium height, wearing rimless glasses and a plaid sport shirt with rolled-up sleeves. His closely trimmed beard mixes the colors of silver and darker steel. The only portion of the room not walled with books—his bioethical library, with the titles on their spines variously in English, Arabic, and Farsi, the language of Iran—is the tall window, in front of which hang pots of philodendron and other plants with cascading leaves. Nor are those three languages the only ones that he commands; he has eleven altogether, including Hindi and his native Gujarati, with modern Turkish the current object of study. He bids me sit in a comfortable recliner, while he stays at his desk, leaning elbows on its surface, sometimes placing his hands, fingers joined, under his chin as he talks. His voice is gentle, sometimes descending into a whisper, but he talks in such a slow, lucid fashion that transcribing the tape of our conversation will be easy.

The basic Muslim position is stated in the Qur'an (3.145): No soul can ever die except by God's will and at a time appointed. Dr. Sachedina asks, "Is it part of the divine plan to cause suffering? With what end?" He offers the story of a once respected, now impoverished sheik who had lost all his friends along with his money. He endured this life as long as he felt that he could, but one day, he tied a rope to a rafter in his room and hung himself. Some people believed that he had indeed done the right thing, to free himself from a life no longer tolerable. Others, however, knew that in escaping one unbearable situation, he had plunged himself into one far worse: the searing fires of Hell. For, by God's ordination, suicide is prohibited. I learn that in Arabic the word for "suicide" is the same as that for "homicide." Both are acts that cannot be retracted, nor is an apology possible. The story illustrates Muslim attitudes on human life and on decision-making in life-and-death issues. As Dr. Sachedina points out, "It underscores the view that the human being has the stewardship not the ownership of his body to enable him to assert his right to handle it the way he pleases. He is merely the caretaker, the real owner being God, the Creator." He adds that instead of considering the refusal of life-support or asking for physician-assisted suicide, a Muslim is obligated to pray for a new opportunity with health regained. In other words, a devout Muslim is better off toughing it out rather than facing the stewpots of Hell.

But this, Dr. Sachedina points out, is a religious evaluation of suffering. It does not give guidance on the issue of the suffering that is caused by illness. Muslims believe that people are the cause of their own suffering and that the way to banish it from the world is through the enactment of good works. I am told that "the patient's 'right to die' cannot be negotiated because, in the first place, life is a divine trust and cannot be terminated by any form of human intervention, and, in the second, its term has been fixed by inalterable divine decree."

Islamic law does not recognize individual autonomy in such matters. Dr. Sachedina says, in his style that frequently omits *the*, *a*, and *an*, "Autonomy—it is unknown in Islamic world. We don't speak about autonomy. Yes, we do speak about individual rights, but as soon as we speak about individual rights, we speak about individual responsibilities. So, rights and obligations are in balance.

I cannot claim my rights as individual if I have not fulfilled my obligations." So, autonomy is not even a matter for abstract discussion because Islam is a religion in which connectedness, one human being to many others—family, neighbors, community—is all important. But, and the exception is all-important, two situations occur in which a terminally ill patient may be allowed to die. One is the relief of pain, in which the medication given not only quells agony but also shortens life. The second is withdrawal of life support, an act viewed as "allowing inevitable death to take its natural course" for someone who has no hope of recovery. Decisions on these matters are not unilateral but rather made through consultation with physician, family, and others involved in the patient's care conferring to determine what course to take. Decision-making is not an individual act but one that is communal, although in Islam it is not only possible but desirable for an individual to make a living will. The will is designed to guide the people who will make the decisions. In no case is the physician giving pain medication or ordering withdrawal of life support considered theologically culpable. In treating to relieve pain, there is no intention to kill, and when respirator and tubes are unplugged, death is seen as caused by the patient's existing disease. Nonetheless, if a family member who stands to inherit money or goods when the patient dies takes part in the decision to withdraw life support, that person is disqualified from inheriting anything, even if the decedent is his or her father.

I ask Dr. Sachedina how he came to be a bioethicist. "I wanted to be a doctor," he says. "I always wanted to be a physician, but our financial situation was not good when my father died." His father's death when he was a boy in Tanzania, his native land, left his mother as the sole provider for seven children. Because going to medical school entailed an impossible expense, he studied humanities in India. When he says he does not know what to call himself, I suggest "doctor of the spirit." He tells me, too, about a touch-point that involves a literal touching. Islam recommends that people go to the graves of their dear ones on Thursday afternoons before the sun sets, and there they are to place a hand, the five fingers outspread, on the grave and dig in, saying a prayer. When his mother died, he was a student in Canada and was unable to return to Tanzania in time for the funeral. "At that point, my heart was so heavy," he says. "As soon as I landed my plane, I went home, took a bath, and wore clean clothes. And I went to the graveyard. I went to her freshly made grave, and I put my fingers on it and wept, and I prayed—then my heart was so light." Now, when he engages in the weekly remembrance of his mother, he goes to his yard in Charlottesville, puts his fingers in the soil, and prays that God grant her His mercy. It is the same great earth, after all, that contains her grave. Before I leave, he gives me an unwitting gift: an objective way to assess quality of life. The Islamic guidelines will be set down in the eponymous chapter, "The Quality of Life."

Dr. Sachedina's well-tutored views on matters of assisted suicide and withdrawal of life-support are seconded by Dr. Hanif Sherali, a native of India who holds an endowed chair of engineering at Virginia Tech in Blacksburg, Virginia. I meet him by a circuitous route: one of my friends refers me to one of her friends who then puts me in touch with Dr. Sherali. He brings out several points in a long, thoughtful communiqué, "Medical Law and Science in Islam." One is the Muslim belief that Allah gives boons to people by afflicting them with sore troubles, which, if they are borne patiently, become expiation for sins and a source of heavenly rewards. "The term 'mercy killing,' he writes, "is a misnomer, and assisted suicide is simply murder! It is indeed *unmerciful* to deprive a person of an opportunity for self-purification."

Dr. Sherali notes two other points bearing on the suffering endured by human beings when they are sick. First, the patient and his or her connections in the world—family, friends, community—are brought closer to God through the power of prayer. Second, the very existence of disease inspires people to seek new medical knowledge, and they are thus benefited not only physically but also spiritually because they gain new appreciation of the munificence of God. The Prophet Muhammad himself urged medical research, for he believed that, in creating diseases, God also created their treatments. The Qur'an and Islamic tradition are rich in documenting both treatments and prescriptions.

Prayer, yes, but Islam also shows a practical side. "First," Dr. Sherali writes, "Islam supports the concept of respecting a patient's prior wishes of not being given certain medications or treatments. A second point is that all knowledge is a gift from Allah." The gift is to be used as Allah has intended—to effect cures or help people bear their illnesses. "However, in a circumstance when there isn't even a minimal chance for any form of self-existence in any capacity, it is futile to use artificial life-support systems. Needless to say, this judgment of essential death must be made with caution and deliberation, but once it is surmised to the best of human abilities that life in any conscious capacity is not possible, it is futile to use support systems to impose an artificial appearance of life." An artificial appearance of life—the situation cannot be more tellingly described.

Islam, Judaism, and the two streams of Christianity, Catholic and Protestant, from which I have sought advice, concur in their beliefs. Suicide, whether self-administered or achieved with help, is forbidden, for to cause one's own death constitutes a human arrogation of a right reserved to God. Buddhism, too, sanctions suicide. Cautioning people to practice virtue by avoiding lust, hate, and ignorance, the Dalai Lama has written, "Realize that by taking a pill or an injection to have a so-called peaceful death you may be depriving yourself of a crucial opportunity for manifesting virtue." But withdrawal of life support is allowed if its use serves merely to put off the inevitable, God-determined moment of death.

I have no credentials in theology, but it occurs to me to wonder, at risk of sacrilege, if deity might not ordain that death be achieved by suicide. I hear the counterargument, that because suicide is divinely prohibited, God cannot put it on the table of possibilities. Yet, I think of the true stories that I've heard of death by choice and of the control that it affords the dying and the comfort that it brings to the survivors. If circumstances had been otherwise, I would indeed have helped my mother kill herself.

CHASING DOWN DEATH—what a slow and stumbling race! Sarah goes downhill in fits and starts, reaching a plateau, then slipping again. The visits from the living decline, for these days Sarah does not always recognize the people who come to see her. She stares at them and frowns, obviously perturbed. But the visits with the dead continue and become more frequent, though Hannah does not figure in them again. Sarah seems to see something, but what? Is she hallucinating? Sadness certainly inhabits the visits, for she cries more often these days. I will learn later that one symptom of dementia is "seeing" people who are not there, and animals, as well. And I hear repeated stories about people nearing death who speak of those who await them on the other side.

Sometimes, these visitants tell you that it is not yet time to die; sometimes, they come to take you with them. She believes in them. I hope that visiting with her mother and sister and husband have given her a kind of comfort that the living can no longer provide. Though she cannot articulate the wish anymore, she seeks to be a rainbow. None of the dead, however, has yet invited her to join them.

The Haunted Woods: Dementia

quem fugis, a, demens? habitarunt di quoque silvas.
What do you run from, you demented soul? Gods
have also lived in these woods.

—Virgil, *Eclogue II*, 60.

TWO AND A HALF YEARS after the first stroke, Sarah's
comprehension is irrecoverably on the wane. Sometimes,
though, she comes through magnificently. She even finds language appropriate to the occasion. One afternoon, Mary, who has
been my friend since our high-school days, comes to town and
spends the night at my house. She has an entourage—two super-
annuated black Labs with well-grizzled muzzles; she supervises
the training of her dogs for field trials, and these two had earned
retirement. One of the visiting animals, a female named Chic, has
ranked in the top ten black Labs in the country at the grand game
of retrieving birds. Dogs and women, we all go to visit my mother.
I'm not sure that she recognizes Mary, whom she had fed and
housed and transported Lord knows how many times, but she
knows that dogs are present. Good old animals, they sit peacefully
on either side of her. She stretches out a hand, and Chic caresses
it with her tongue. "Lick, lick," Sarah says. "Lick, lick." Her face
lights up with pleasure. And with a wiggle of her fingers, she

summons her own little white dog, which is dwarfed by these black giants. On another day, though she does not grace the occasion with language, she also mightily enjoys the potluck party that we hold in her living and dining rooms to celebrate her eighty-fifth birthday. The center of attention from children, grandchildren, and at least three of the nine great-grands, she beams.

But ask Sarah if she'd like peaches for lunch, and she'll say, "Yes," give her a choice between peaches and applesauce, she'll also say, "Yes." At this time she is infinitely agreeable. She may not have understood the first question, however, and she certainly cannot make choices. So, we who are close at hand must choose for her. Peaches, yes; applesauce, no, or perhaps the other way around, depending on the state of the kitchen cupboards. Biopsy, yes; mastectomy, no, not even if the lump had been cancerous.

I begin to believe that the most important task of family and caregivers is to do all that we can to keep Sarah comfortable and smiling and to ward off any talk, any actions that might frighten her. Rosa has installed a monitor so that the caregivers may listen to her breathing when she sleeps. Any restlessness, any cries will bring immediate attention. And should pain strike, it can be tamed and gentled with one or more of the many magic potions in the modern pharmacopoeia. I know now that had the lump proved malignant, I might have had to do battle to keep my mother from the surgeon's knife. My nomination in her living will as her decision-maker is not legally sufficient to give my word authority. There are family members who earnestly believe that removal of cancerous tissue is better than living with the disease. Deciding what to do is made difficult, if not impossible, if family and caretakers disagree. But I am sure that the pertinent question is, Which is the better course for a frail, increasingly incompetent woman in her mid-eighties—quelling the pain of a malignancy or relieving the pain entailed by recovering from amputative surgery, not to mention the fear that hospitalization would cause?

There are two means to approach decision-making on behalf of someone who cannot do so. One is known as substituted judgment, and the other, as best interests. The former involves putting yourself in the place of the person who is incompetent and settling on what you believe that person would have wanted. Sometimes, supportive evidence—a living will or even a letter outlining wishes—is necessary for this kind of judgment to hold force. Making a decision according to best interests entails considering the benefits and drawbacks of care, the risks, the possible pain, and the treatment's potential to alleviate a problem or bring back good health. For my mother, there is no return to health. But if the mastectomy issue had come to the fore, I would have used both standards as a base for my opinion against it. She'd always been shy of doctors and hospitals. I know she would have wanted to avoid them both. And, at her age, in her damaged condition, amputation seemed an option far more burdensome and painful than comfort care.

MY MOTHER is lost in a haunted woods rarely illuminated by daylight, and there's no coming back to the sun, no return to the bustle and the bucolic vistas of her former life. Dementia—the very word brings prickles to the back of my neck. It's also an honest word, for its Latin translates as "away from the mind, out of the mind."

Only a small percentage of old people become demented. In 2002, as I write, 35 million people over the age of sixty-five live in the United States—that's twelve percent of the country's population (and I am one of them). The group aged eighty and up is the part of our society with the highest rate of growth. In 2020, the population of over-sixty-fives is expected to amount to seventeen percent of people living in the U.S. But of today's 35 million, only two-and-a-half million—seven and a half percent—suffer from increasingly severe dementia that may be amenable to medication but cannot be cured. Most of these people live in the community rather than in hospitals or nursing homes. Nor are all dementias the same. They vary in their causes and effects, as well as in their susceptibility to treatment. The chances of being afflicted with any kind of dementia increase dramatically with age. It is estimated that fifteen to twenty percent of people over seventy-five are affected, and twenty-five to an astounding fifty percent of those over eighty-five. So, when the number of people over eighty-five increases, as certainly it shall, the number of those who become demented will also burgeon.

The Alzheimer's type is the most common dementia, affecting some sixty-five percent of people who lose their intellectual capacity. It begins with a snowballing increase in forgetful senior moments, and it progresses slowly but inexorably, eroding the victim's ability to think and understand. It cannot be cured, though its development may be retarded with drugs and activities that stimulate the patient's thoughts and feelings. As one specialist told me in regard to such activities, "People get worse less fast." Other dementias arise from head injuries, which occur suddenly and may improve greatly with healing; yet others, from many small strokes (multi-infarct dementia); or, as with Sarah, one or two major strokes exacerbated by mini-strokes (vascular dementia). They stem, too, from Parkinson's disease, in which dementia is common, or from such problems as vitamin B12 deficiency, hypothyroidism, and kidneys that work inefficiently, allowing toxins to pile up in the blood. Still others are engendered by maladies such as HIV infection, AIDS, syphilis, and Creutzfeldt-Jakob disease, a variant of the bovine ailment known as mad cow disease. They may also be brought into being by overconsumption of alcohol or drugs.

Dementia, whatever its etiology, is not a disease in itself but rather a congeries of symptoms characterized in every last case by a memory that's gone glimmering, especially in regard to events in the recent or immediate past. Without memory impairment, there is no dementia. That impairment is inevitably accompanied by personality changes and one or more of these disabilities: aphasia, apraxia, agnosia, anomie, and difficulties with executive functioning. Put into plain English, *aphasia* means partial or complete loss of speech; sometimes it is global, with the patient both unable to speak and to understand what someone else says. *Apraxia* is a damaged ability to perform complex, coordinated muscular movements—chewing, swallowing, tooth-brushing, and forget about dancing the fandango or driving a car. *Agnosia* refers to bafflement when it comes to recognizing people, objects, and stimuli that should be familiar. A cousin comes to visit, or a long-time friend; either may be greeted with puzzled scowls. A banana, a piece of toast, and other things long part of the patient's diet will receive the same treatment. The ring of a telephone, the shriek of a fire siren may set off panic. As for *anomie,* it's an agitated restlessness that comes from lack of purpose, from loss of control over actions and events. Finally, when executive functioning wanes, a person loses the ability to plan ahead, to make and follow through on appointments, and to anticipate the arrival of family or friends; organizational skills also fall by the wayside, from making shopping lists and straightening out dresser drawers to more complex tasks like reconciling bank statement with checkbook and preparing schedules. Dementia may also involve a disturbing phenomenon colorfully known as "sundowning," in which the onset of dusk and night exacerbates fears and causes agitation. As Sarah lives on, her failing memory is accompanied by the whole troupe of these stuttering, stumbling companions, from speechlessness to evening unrest. But, unlike an Alzheimer's patient, she typifies the person suffering from vascular dementia in that she has managed to retain much of her old, outgoing personality.

Other conditions sometimes mimic dementia. Chief among them is depression, along with bipolar disorder, the au courant term for manic depression. People lost in the abyss of severe depression may be said to be suffering from a pseudodementia, which some clinicians prefer to call simply the dementia of depression. Another mimic is delirium, which may cause the mood-swings and impairments typical of dementia. For this condition, there's usually an underlying medical cause—an infection, pneumonia, an event in the central nervous system like a hematoma, or simply a change in medication.

How to sort it all out?

If there's a severe and sudden change, with someone going from rationality to bizarre behavior in a short time, the emergency room may be the place of choice to start discovering what's wrong. But most dementias are more insidious, starting with symptoms that are visible only with hindsight, then progressing gradually but inexorably. The terrain is often that of slopes and plateaus. The sufferer slides downhill, then attains a temporary stasis; symptoms become more severe, though perhaps only slightly so, then level off. But sooner or later, it becomes apparent that the demons of dementia are at work, tunneling like sappers through long-established ways of thinking and acting. The family doctor is the person who may best begin to assess the problem. The tools for assessment are many: a history taken from the patient or the family; physical and neurological exams; evaluation of the patient's mental state; blood tests; a metabolic profile; a CT scan or an MRI. The family practitioner may call on specialists, like psychiatrists, neurologists, and neuropsychologists, all of whom may help to differentiate one dementia from another or from its mimics. The process is one of elimination, a sorting out to see whether the condition is treatable. Why find out? Not just to discover if treatment is possible but because, if true dementia exists, each form has its own array of symptoms and its own set of strategies for management. In each situation, caregivers need to know how best to help and to interpret the messages that even those with gaping holes in memory and behavior are able to deliver.

Communication between a person who is rational and one who is not—how might that work? When I ask my mother's physician, James LaGrua, who treats a number of demented patients, he gives a doctor's point of view. "It all depends how far you are in the dementia. A person can have mild to moderate dementia and still make decisions. You may not be able to balance your checkbook, but you can still say what you want done to your body. We look at those decisions as being really fundamental. And with moderate dementia, we will ask them because we believe that they have credit to say what they want and don't want. We try to answer those questions before the dementia is severe. As it becomes severe, we will try, if we have a relationship with the family, to establish how far we're going to go with care." So, gentle conversations held early on may constitute a vital element in knowing what a somewhat fuzzy-minded person wants.

Nonverbal messages are also an essential part of the vocabulary of both patient and caregiver. Even a badly impaired person can detect the six basic facial expressions: happiness, sadness, anger, fear, surprise, and disgust. Gestures, too, figure in this kind of communication, along with tone of voice and touch. Equally, someone who suffers from a dementia of any kind is also able not just to read the nonverbal signs but to deliver them. And if we who are still in the light understand these messages, then we can keep the bewildered from wandering and from catastrophic confusion; we can more easily comfort them.

BUT HOW DO you find the best care for someone who is truly demented? A friend refers me to a woman I'll call Alexis, whose mother had Alzheimer's disease. (I've given pseudonyms to all the people in this account to protect their privacy.) We meet at Alexis's house, newly inherited from her parents and filled with chinoiserie and other orientalia—lotus-decorated plates, a pair of brass elephant bookends, calligraphic ornamentation on a huge breakfront. In her early fifties, plump and brown-eyed, with her naturally curly hair streaked with gray over her forehead, she herself is delightfully casual and articulate. The house is also home to her brother Harold, and to two large dogs gleefully swishing their furry tails as I walk in the door and sit down. One is a shedding Siberian husky with eyes the blue of a glacial lake; the other, a retriever of sorts named Rockbridge for the county in which Alexis found her as a skin-and-bones stray with a ratty tail. Seven years ago, Alexis stopped at the sight of a dog lying by the side of the road, then moved on, only to find that the dog was racing after her car. There was no choice but to stop again and take the dog on board. And Alexis's mother, Flora, fell in love with the animal, which had been brought straight to the parental home. When Alexis suggested that it was time to take her new dog to her own home, Flora would say in an offhand way that Rocky needed a bit more time with her. "I finally realized that my mother wanted my dog," Alexis says. "What could I do but give her the dog?" The love affair was mutual, dog and woman, and lasted until Flora's death.

At the time that Rocky arrived, Flora had already been diagnosed with the early stages of Alzheimer's. "She was spacey, anyway, a bit of an airhead," Alexis says, "but she had stopped doing the household bills and wouldn't cook—she hated cooking to begin with." Then, in 1996, Alexis's father, Jerome, had a severe stroke, which left him partially aphasic and immobile. Long-standing diabetes compounded the problem. After some in-hospital rehab, he went to Blue Sky Manor, where a determined therapist got him up and walking. While he was there, he also acquired a nasty bedsore. Alexis describes his medical care as "pretty poor." She says, "In this situation, you have to learn how to raise a ruckus." When he returned home, Alexis stayed with her parents at night, while Harold was at hand during the day. It soon became evident that the two of them could not handle care by themselves—and that more help was needed, especially with both parents ill. Alexis's job with student medical services at a university made for a seventy-mile commute every day. She and Harold soon hired a housekeeper for the daytime hours, while the two of them took turns at night caring for their parents. The housekeeper was found through social services at the hospital where Jerome had been taken after his stroke. Alexis issues a caution here: "You need to be careful when hiring. Check out the local market for wages. Don't do something financially bad." As it happened, the housekeeper lived in another town where the wage rates for her job were considerably higher. But she was more than competent.

Then, nine months later, Jerome had what Alexis describes as "a monster stroke," which left him unable to swallow. As a result, when he was fed, food would be aspirated into his lungs, and over and again, he'd end up in the hospital with pneumonia. I ask Alexis if she and Harold had ever considered letting him die rather than rushing him to the hospital, she says, "I wasn't there. It was an automatic reflex of the housekeeper to call 911." The upshot was implantation of a tube in his stomach, even though he had earlier indicated to the doctor that he didn't want one. Flora, however, was adamant, believing that there would be a miracle. "It was not rational thinking," Alexis says. With intubation, round-the-clock care was in order. To find caregivers, she placed ads in the local paper, conducted countless interviews, and checked references. Juggling the demands of both parental care and her job, she found herself under great stress, with the result that she left her university job for one in the private sphere. "But the lesson is," she says, "not to start something new when you are seventy-five percent distracted."

When the tube first went in, Jerome's doctor gave him a prognosis of six months to live, and hospice was called in. Six months, however, stretched into nearly four-and-a-half years of care day and night. The first tube lasted a good nine months, and hospice care ceased. "We were kicked out of hospice most unceremoniously," Alexis recalls. It seems that having a second tube implanted gave the signal that the family had opted for life rather than a good death. "Then hospice leaves you because it's no longer palliative care." Later, oxygen and suctioning equipment were added to the mechanical devices keeping Jerome alive. Although he could not speak nor walk, his mind remained intact, and he could signal his wishes and feelings to those around him. Along with the hired caregivers, Alexis and Harold took full shifts.

During this time, Flora was becoming progressively more demented, though she remained completely mobile. Alexis describes

her as "a sweet demented person," but it nonetheless became necessary to keep the house free of plants for Flora would water them
and also the furniture on which they'd been placed. Doors were
locked—the doors that lead outside and the door that led into the
refrigerator for Flora would empty it out to feed Rockbridge—"a
carryover of nurturing behavior," according to Alexis. "Once she
gave Rocky a whole beef roast." Flora hated the limitations of
locked doors and once tried to retrieve the refrigerator key from
Alexis's hand. Flora grabbed the thumb of the hand that held the
key and said that she'd break it if her daughter did not yield.
Alexis kept the key, but the incident caused her to make "a
mental divorce from my mother," who had never in the past even
thought of hurting her children, much less actually done so. But,
as Alexis knows, Flora was no longer a thinking person.

"She went back to her childhood," Alexis says, "and enjoyed
childish things." When the very young children of Alexis's
friends came visiting along with their mothers, Flora would get
down on the floor to play with them. And Flora was given toys of
her own—stuffed animals, dolls, crayons, and coloring books.
Loving anything with bright lights, she was mesmerized by a
small artificial fiber-optic Christmas tree that showed an aurora of
shimmering, shifting colors on the ends of its needles when
plugged in. Another favorite was a fake aquarium, with bubbles
rising and colorful artificial fish darting through the water. One
of the caregivers, a tender-hearted young woman who'd catch
moths in the house and set them free outside, played games with
her. Alexis remembers them engaging in "I spy with my little
eye." The caregiver would name the color, red or green or blue,
and Flora would try to guess which object had been spied.

People would ask Alexis if it wasn't truly heartbreaking when
her mother didn't recognize her and were astonished when she
told them, "No." Alexis says it was interesting to figure out just

who Flora thought she was. Often she was perceived as Flora's sister. Once, when she was asked getting-to-know-you questions, it was clear that Flora saw her as a new caregiver. When Flora heard that Alexis lived in Charlottesville, she said, "Oh, you must know my daughter." Indeed!

As the years passed, Flora became physically weaker. She could not bathe or dress herself, and she became incontinent. But she could walk through the house if she had help. Alexis says, "It was like having an early toddler who can't do more than a few steps without landing on her bottom." Near the end, Flora would state over and again that she wanted to go home. Alexis does not interpret this desire as an indication that her mother was getting ready to die but read it rather as a wish to return to the home of her childhood, the top story of a four-story brick house, which now comprises the offices of a law firm in the heart of town. In Flora's day it held four generations of her family. Alexis says that Flora seemed to see the people who had lived there. At the end, Flora was less connected with the living than with family members long dead. She was, however, fully aware of Jerome, her husband for sixty years, whose understanding of speech had not been destroyed by his strokes. She would talk to him and kiss him. The bond, begun in the 1940s during World War II, remained strong.

I ask Alexis how she learned to deal with her mother's dementia. She did go to the local chapter of the Alzheimer's Association for literature but did not join a support group. The literature proved helpful, for it contained such tips as putting food on plain plates, not heavily decorated ones, so that it was easy to see. But for the most part, Alexis and Harold were given on-the-job training. I ask if the six-plus years of caring for not one but both parents has in any way changed her life.

"I changed my career path totally," she says. She now lives in the parental home and telecommutes, working for a medical publishing company. And she has made out a living will. Because she and Harold, neither of them married, have long discussed what each wants in the way of end-of-life health-care—no tubes, no heroic measures—she has not made a DPA but recognizes that doing so is in the cards, for the day will come when only one of them is left alive.

Jerome died in August, 2002; Flora, also in August, a short nine days later. Jerome's death had long been planned—"an exit strategy," as Alexis puts it. The time came that the nutritive formula delivered through the tube disagreed with him, nor could it be easily adjusted without considerable experimentation. The feeding tube was removed, and Jerome was given morphine injections to allay any pain. He died four days later. Flora died in her sleep, probably of heart failure for she'd had several earlier bouts with cardiac distress. I marvel that Alexis is able to tell me so calmly about their deaths and the six years leading up to their final moments. But she tells me what I know by heart, that she and Harold did their grieving long before their parents died. Both have been cremated and now rest in the hall closet. Alexis and her brother plan to bury the ashes in the yard of the house their parents loved and to host a major celebration on that occasion—food, drink, memorial remarks, stories, and, best of all, laughter.

"I've talked your ear off," Alexis says as I prepare to leave. "No," I tell her, "you've been generous." And I think of all that she did right to help her mother—keeping Flora safe, responding to her childlike self with games, toys, and lights, providing a dog to love, and making sure that husband and wife stayed together.

LATER I talk with one of Jerome's caregivers, who asks that I call her Debra. She is a slight, silver-haired woman in her early sixties.

I've known her for some years now because she is also a four-year veteran of my mother's team. Sitting in my kitchen, occasionally sipping iced tea, she defines a caregiver's role: "First, you have to give your patients lots of respect. You have to treat them as if their mind is still good, even though sometimes it's not. You have to be very gentle. You follow all the doctors' orders in regard to medicines. And talk to them, communicate with them. Don't stop with just using your nursing skills." It was Debra who picked up on reading to my mother, using her voice as a clear, soothing music, after I'd let the stories lapse. She tells me how important communication was with Jerome, who could not speak and respond but did comprehend speech and also knew his own plight. "He had to be cared for just like a baby," Debra says. "He knew that he had soiled the bed. I took care of him, and that was a delicate, awkward procedure with him. But after a little while, I would talk to him during the process. So, it got to be easier. Sometimes, it's so much better if they don't really know what's going on when they get to this state." And Debra tells me that before she came along, Harold was giving his diabetic father insulin shots in a fairly rough, untrained way. So, Debra took on that job. And she tells of the restraint in regard to food that she and the other caregivers practiced to help Jerome: "He was doing very well on the nutrients, the milk shakes, they were giving him. But we were careful not to mention food and careful not to eat in the room where he was. When any television program came on that had anything to do with food, we muted the sound so that he couldn't hear it. That was a sad situation, for even though you can't eat, you know the body wants to."

Debra tells me then of her current job as one of a round-the-clock team caring for a woman I'll call Mrs. Morgan, who is afflicted with Parkinson's and a form of dementia. I ask how she handles someone in that condition. "With Mrs. Morgan, you make suggestions. You don't ever tell her what to do. You watch after her without her really knowing that you are there. If she goes out for a walk, she doesn't know that I'm right behind her. But I make sure that she's all right because there are several times that she's fallen. I need to be there to help her. And she'd say, 'Where did you come from?' And I say, 'I thought I'd go for a walk, too.' Psychology—you have to manage her without her knowing that you're helping her. She's on antidepressants, and I think she's in constant pain. She's a very difficult case."

Debra also outlines another sort of difficulty, one that must grind a caregiver in the way that a millstone crushes grain: conflicting aims within a patient's family. She speaks of another patient whose children were at loggerheads about their grievously debilitated mother's care. It's the all-too-common story of one hoping that the dark prince will soon arrive, while the other opts for doing everything to stave off death. "We caregivers were torn," Debra says, "because we were told to do one thing by one member of the family and something totally different by another member. Finally, we had to make our own judgment."

We come full circle back to the importance of communication, but not just between caregiver and family, no, for everyone, every last soul, connected with an impending death—spouse, children, nurses, aides, physicians—needs to arrive at a consensus. Granted, doing so does not prevent mistakes, but it surely makes for a more clear-headed joint effort at taking the best possible course, given the information available. Forgetting our latter-day reticence to speak of death, we must talk, talk, and keep on talking.

Debra and I reminisce then about my mother. She tells me that Sarah, even in the depths of dementia, was able to acknowledge Debra's help in ways that needed no words. "Sometimes," she says, "Sarah would just look up at you and there was this glimmer in her eyes of appreciation. If you would just do little things, maybe bring her a piece of candy, though you'd know she didn't need it, then she'd give you a sweet look."

Listening to her, looking back at the care she gave my mother, I think that Debra is an ideal aide, cheerful, smiling, and patient, ever calm in voice and demeanor, able to comfort her patients with her soothing presence, and never treating them as less than her equal, no matter how great the disrepair of their bodies and minds. She is infinitely giving. Her responsibilities are huge, including overseeing her patient's nutrition, medications, and safety. And she is trained to a T as a certified nursing assistant (CNA) in necessary nursing skills, to which she adds several decades of experience. Her focus as a caregiver is life, of course, but if so instructed, she would let a dying patient slip away, while doing her best to assure comfort. But, oh, what hard work, what physically and mentally challenging hard work it is to be a caregiver! Debra has contributed humbling insights.

COMMUNICATIONS: Though Alexis didn't use the available resources to help her with caring for a demented mother, except to gather reading material on Alzheimer's disease, they do exist, and in more forms than just the Alzheimer's Association. It should be noted that the Alzheimer's Association can serve as a source of support for those of us who are faced with other dementias. On the local level, the family physician is the person with whom to start. Then, many communities have programs or agencies that pay special attention to the needs of old people. My small town, Staunton, with a population of about 22,000, offers access to information and programs serving the elderly through the Valley Program for

Aging Services, a public agency of a sort found nationwide. Adult daycare centers have also become more common, offering hours of respite to exhausted caregivers. Regional hospitals, too, may offer workshops that help caregivers understand dementia in its protean guises and to learn how best to deal with it, whatever form it takes. Home-care agencies are also connected with these hospitals; the nurses and aides on the staff may offer not only insights but suggestions on sources of information. Some private home-care service providers, like the franchise operations Home Instead Senior Care and Visiting Angels, which deal primarily with elderly adults who are competent but in need of companionable assistance in shopping, driving, cooking, and other household tasks, may also take on demented patients for an hour or two so that we, the primary caregivers, can catch our breath. One such franchise, ComForcare, advertises that its employees are trained to care for people with Alzheimer's and other dementias. Nationally, many groups can steer us in a productive direction. Among them are the National Council on Aging and Aging Network Services, the latter of which lists private care managers nationwide—trained counselors and geriatric social workers who can help with organizing care for an older, incompetent person. The groups that I have found most supportive and useful are listed in an appendix on resources.

The time may well come when caring for an older, demented person, or for one who is not demented but frail and tetchy, takes on critical mass for the caregiver—extreme weariness, failing physical stamina, loss of control over your own life. Alexis tells me that it was good to be able to keep her mother at home, but then, for Alexis's parents, the costs of twenty-four-hour care seven days a week were affordable, though not without sacrifice. It was necessary, as Jerome's caregiver Debra told me, for Alexis to sell some valuable possessions to maintain the cash flow for home care. After her father died, she and Harold did consider placing Flora in a nursing home, but that idea came to naught when Flora's death occurred a little over a week after Jerome's. Nonetheless, I know that nursing-home care for one or both would have been far less extravagant than paying for six years' worth of home care. If constant vigilance is required, but a caregiver is stretched too thin to provide it, then putting a patient in a nursing home is—not "seems to be," but *is*—a reasonable move. Many of us are still left in a bind, however, for we cannot afford a nursing facility, much less round-the-clock care at home. It's up to us to explore every possible local, regional, and national resource, and to do so well before a crisis occurs.

BUT HOW HARD it is to plan! How nearly impossible! The dark woods of dementia are filled with frightening uncertainties for both the one losing rationality and those who must watch it happen. Marguerite (as I'll call her), a middle-school guidance counselor living in Connecticut, contacts me on the recommendation of a mutual friend. She writes a cautionary tale about her husband, Eric. In his prime, he was an accomplished composer and church musician, not only playing organs to critical praise but also designing them. Among many other distinguished positions, he served as Master of the Choristers at the Cathedral of St. John the Divine in New York City and was later the coordinator of the Standing Commission on Church Music of the Episcopal Church. Twenty-six years older than she, he is now eighty. She says that he is not completely irrational these days but has reached the point at which he cannot make decisions. Dementia, she says, "has come upon him fairly slowly, and I guess it is similar to living with someone who is losing or gaining weight. The changes are so gradual that one hardly notices. But he is diminished." After she had noticed that he was becoming less capable in many respects, including the ability to drive safely, she did nothing at first. Only when someone who had met him for the first time exclaimed, "That man is *driving*?" did she take steps to get him off the road. Fortunately, their family doctor told Eric that he could no longer drive, and Marguerite hid the car keys. She says that he did not seem to mind being grounded but that if the keys had been available, he would have used them, forgetting that he was not supposed to drive. Turning his driver's license in to the Department of Motor Vehicles brought a surprise: their auto insurance rates jumped dramatically, for their teen-aged son, Carl, was now the primary driver of his father's car.

Eric also has problems with breathing and mobility. "I suspect," Marguerite says, "if he were not limited mobility-wise, he would be a wanderer. As it is, he doesn't have the ability to leave the house on his own." Nor can he engage these days in serious conversation. She thinks he forgets what's being talked about. More troublesome is his response to telephone calls. Marguerite's work in two middle schools, a job she relishes, entails leaving Eric alone at home for most of the day. When telemarketers call, he may make arrangements to use their services. A chimney sweep arrived out of the blue, as did an insurance policy on Carl's life. Marguerite says, "Once I returned home to this: 'I had a devil of a time finding your Social Security number today.' When I asked him why he needed it, he replied, 'Well, I didn't, but someone called here and they wanted it.'"

The future casts shadows on Marguerite's thinking. She says that Eric does not grumble, that he deals gracefully with his aging and the concomitant problems. He is easy to care for. But, as

Marguerite tells me, "The time is coming, I know, when he will not be able to be alone at all, and I worry about that and about the financial impact it will have on us. Neither he nor I have long-term-care insurance. This may be my denial acting up again or it may be my Scarlett O'Hara attitude—but I'm not going to think about that right now."

There shall be burdens, but she'll shoulder them, in large part because she has been blessed with optimism and a deep faith in God. And Carl will surely help when needed; she describes him as having inherited a double dose of genes—half from his maternal grandparents and half from his father—for kindness, goodness, and an even temperament. Nonetheless, her story may serve as a wake-up reminder that the issues of aging can be faced head-on before decrepitude and witlessness set in.

SARAH'S DEMENTIA is vascular, the result of the strokes, which have damaged her brain beyond recovery. She will never emerge from the God-haunted woods. And we are lost with her, for we, too, have entered terra incognita. Though we recognize what I'll later understand as a typical pattern for vascular dementia—plateaus, then a sudden change, followed by a new plateau—her illness is baffling. It is up to us, family and caregivers, to keep her safe so long as she shall live. But having no guidelines, no rules of thumb, we follow a course of by-guess-and-by-golly. Our mistakes become apparent only after they're made.

One mistake is taking her to the dentist for a filling. She regularly visits a hygienist to have her teeth cleaned. Such a routine was part of her old life, and it now seems to cause her no distress. Her teeth have been extraordinarily healthy—no cavities, no gum disease. But one day Rosa discovers a spot of decay as she brushes

Sarah's teeth. My mother exhibits no signs of pain, she does not wince or grunt when the tooth is touched, but arrangements are made to have the spot cleaned out and filled.

How can you tell if a confused, speechless person is in pain? The clues lie in the onset of behavior that is not customary. Faces often lose serenity; telltale expressions like frowns or grimaces replace a calm mien. Eyes may be squinched tightly shut or blink rapidly. Voices become instruments that call for help with a repertoire ranging from sighs and moans through shrieks or profanity that somehow bursts forth on such occasions. Posture may change, too, going from relaxed to rigid. The person in pain may exhibit agitation, rock back and forth, or show a diminished ability to walk or eat. Do tears well where once there were smiles? Does confusion deepen? Where once an appetite was hearty, food and drink may be refused. There may be alterations in the rhythms of sleeping and waking. Any deviation from ordinary behavior can signal pain. And it may help to note if pain seems to be occurring when there's movement, as during transfers from bed to chair, or when there is little or no movement because the irrational person is sitting or lying down. In other words, you follow the rules for assessing pain in a pet. You read the signs as best you can.

Sarah finds a way to deliver a nonverbal message expressing her wishes when she is seated in the dentist's chair. A ray of light—small and faint but light nonetheless—enters the dark, haunted woods of her understanding. It may have been an awareness that the dentist is unfamiliar or that she is in a room not like the one in which her close-to-perfect teeth are regularly cleaned by a dental hygienist. Whatever the reason, she tightens her face, locks her jaw, and obstinately refuses to let the dentist so much as take an x-ray. No attempt at explanation, no pleading moves her. She makes it perfectly clear that no one on this particular day in this particular place will be allowed to mess with her mouth. After she is back at home, sitting in her recliner, I discuss the situation with Rosa, who accompanied my mother to the dentist's office. Rosa wants to try again. I think not, and her physician agrees. My mother is able to draw amply from a well of stubbornness. I suspect that the event holds a lesson: Do not try to fix what she doesn't want fixed. She may well have a cavity. It may bring pain. But pain is something that can be dealt with. With her doctor's help, I begin to understand that comfort, not cure, is the best that we can do.

We can keep her from hurting. We can make sure that she has a routine, for she is calm when events happen every day in a predictable order: rising, toileting and bathing, breakfast, recliner-time, lunch, a postprandial snooze that may last an hour or two, rising again, more recliner-time, dinner, evening television, and early to bed. She is like a pet that becomes visibly distressed when habits change. It is not that she cannot adjust to new people, things, and situations but rather that she does it slowly and ever more slowly. I entertain the thought that we are blessed because she cannot walk and therefore cannot wander.

But where do we go from here?

Hospice

Has anyone supposed it lucky to be born?
I hasten to inform him or her, it is just as lucky
to die, and I know it.

—Walt Whitman, "Song of Myself, 7"

ON A MORNING in early May, 1997, Rosa telephones. "Sarah won't open her mouth, her eyes are shut tight. We can't get any food or fluid down her."

I ask how long it's been since my mother closed down.

"Since last night. But it don't take long for a body to lose strength."

"What do you suggest?"

"Get her to the hospital, sooner the better. Call the doctor, will you." It's not a question but rather a command. "Tell him what's up. He'll get her admitted, and she can be fed."

Before I put in the call, I go to see her. Her face is locked, jaw clenched and eyes squinched tightly together. She's making her body express what she cannot put into words. She's working as hard as flesh and bone will let her to thrust off the world's quotidian demands. I pat her hand. She winces in a way that signals, "Leave me alone!" In a remote, unthinking way, she must feel that she has regained some control over the course of her life.

Rosa hovers hugely and says, "She worries me, not eating, not drinking. Hospital is the way to get the nourishment into her."

A tube threaded through her nose to her stomach, an IV in her hand—the images are appalling, but I promise to let Rosa know what the young doctor with the gold-brown eyes says the moment that he and I finish talking. We'll abide by his advice.

A busy man, Dr. LaGrua does not return my call until late afternoon. But when we do connect, it is as if only my mother and her problem are of concern. And he confirms my notion that she's trying to tell us something. "No hospital," he says. "It's not uncommon for an old person just to shut down. They refuse to eat, they refuse to see, they withdraw into themselves. And it's a peaceful way to die. In most cases death comes without any pain at all. For a few people, though, the bowels become occluded, and that can hurt. But we have medication to ease the discomfort." And I learn the reason that death occurs: without food and water, the body's electrolyte balance is altered to such an extent that a patient becomes anesthetized and just closes down, floating away in a painless sleep. The process might be compared to running out of gas.

Care that keeps Sarah comfortable, strictly palliative care— that's what he's suggesting, not care that tries to cure. I think back on all the rescues that have been performed in the past three-and-a-half years—Dilantin to keep my mother's seizures at bay, antihistamines to prevent sinus problems and wheezes, antibiotics to control the everlasting, catheter-caused urinary-tract infections and, recently, to snatch her back from the brink of pneumonia. Pneumonia is said to be the old person's friend; it could have been hers. The only drug I'd like to see continued is the Dilantin, for it can propitiate the seizures that fill her brimful of shuddering fear.

"Dilantin's fine," he says. "Anything else can be prescribed as need be. I think she's a good candidate now for hospice care."

In other words, he believes that she will live, at most, for six more months. And we make arrangements with the hospice headquartered at the regional hospital to provide its services, not just for her but also for the rest of us—her family, her caregivers, her friends. She'll stay at home throughout and die not in some strange hospital contraption but in her own sweet bed, an antique that looks like a big double sleigh.

Carol, one of the nurses affiliated with the hospice, comes to see us. My mother is settled in her bed for an after-lunch nap—Rosa did manage to feed her a few bites. The monitor in the den carries the sounds of her slow, heavy breathing. Bob, the younger of my two brothers, his wife, and their son sit amid bright cushions on the daybed. Rosa has summoned them. She herself, glowering, occupies the swivel chair at the desk. She has already expressed her reservations about the hospice idea; though she does not put it into so many words, I know that she fears that her job will be threatened or brought to an end by strangers invading the territory that she's claimed for four and a half years. But as Carol outlines the program, the glower relaxes. Sarah will remain at home, surrounded by her family and caregiving trio. The hospice will provide experienced backup, answering our questions, providing drugs for Sarah in case of pain, and helping us deal with her dying.

I walk with Carol to her car. "Your brother's not comfortable with this," she says. I agree with her that he and his family have been in a state of denial, that the advent of hospice into our mother's waning days is a signal as strong as a flashing Mars light and a siren: Death is coming. Carol hopes that she'll be able to convey to them that the hospice serves the living, not just those approaching the end but also the rest of us who have years of triumph and sorrow ahead of us. My mother is still in this world but not of it, and the looming of her death is, at best, unsettling to live with. It is as if the family's lives have been put on hold. But hospice will ease our way as well as hers.

HOSPICE—the very word sets off visions of snowy mountaintops, along with St. Bernards toting small casks of brandy on their collars and bearded monks leading rescued alpinists out of crevasses, out of avalanches into safety. The root of the word is the Latin *hospes,* which means "guest," "host," and "stranger." It applies to someone invited, to the person issuing the invitation, and also to a stranger who arrives out of the blue to be sheltered and fed. Hospital, hotel, and hospitality also spring from *hospes*: first, the places in which strangers are cared for, and then, the amenities, the friendship that a host may offer to a guest, be the guest an old acquaintance or someone never seen before. And safety is, I think, a crucial aspect of the initial concept and its ramifications: protection of the sojourner, who may be a pilgrim, a traveler for business or pleasure, or someone like my mother, sojourning in the house of life and approaching its last door. A hospice will take her in for this last stage of her journey and care for her tenderly.

The idea of hospice as a shelter for the terminally ill became reality in 1948—only a blip of time ago—when Dr. Cicely Saunders founded St. Christopher's Hospice, a live-in facility, in London. At-home services did not come into being for twenty-six more years, in 1974. That's the year that the first hospice in the United States was founded. The Connecticut Hospice located in New Haven, opened its arms to people vitally engaged in the act of dying. Today, hospices offer end-of-life care to an omnium-gatherum of patients. The Zen Hospice Project in San Francisco was founded in 1987 on Buddhist principles, but it cares not just for true believers but also for anyone of any faith (or lack of faith) who seeks compassion at the end of life. There are also hospices that focus on prison inmates, and even hospices for pets.

No matter their leanings, hospices come in an array of shapes and forms. Some are nonprofit, while others aim to make money. Some are independent and community-based, while others are affiliated with existing institutions, like hospitals. Hospices may be licensed by the state in which they're located, although not every state has legislation authorizing such licensure, and they may also be federally certified. Such certification allows the hospice to treat patients covered by Medicare and Medicaid and to collect payment from those entities. The form known as a "support hospice" is staffed solely by volunteers and is not often found today, though in the past, it was common. All hospices of any kind rely on volunteers as well as professional staff. Medicare, in fact, mandates that five percent of the services rendered by a certified hospice must be delivered by volunteers. And all hospices have the same goals: to ameliorate disease and relieve pain, to provide ongoing physical care, to assure patients and their families that they will not face death without comfort and support, and to offer coping skills to the bereaved. It's amply clear that people do not want to die in the absence of caring company. All hospices share the same watchword: compassion. What they strive to bring to patients is a peaceful dying, which St. Benedict long ago called *transitus*—a crossing-place and, by extension, the passage from one condition to another. Every hospice is also magnificently able to adapt its program to serve individual needs—no one-size-fits-all here. The old person who is demented requires something other than the person who is sound of mind but not of body. A report issued in November, 2002, by Last Acts, a coalition of health-care professionals, gives a telling statistic: only 24.9 percent of Americans die at home, while 70 percent would like to do so. Hospice programs, be they private or in a hospital, are all designed to help the 70 percent attain their wish.

In 1997, only 14 percent of those who could qualify for hospice care were actually served, nor has the percentage improved significantly since then. Two factors contribute to the pitifully low use of such care. One is sheer ignorance not only of actual hospices but also of the concept. The other is money. Charitable contributions can make or break a hospice: if they come in, the hospice will be financially healthy, able to meet needs beyond those paid for by Medicare or other insurance, but without donations, a hospice can be pushed swiftly into financial crisis. But no one in need is ever turned away. Oh, mortality—*media vita, in morte sumus,* in the midst of life, we are caught in death. Hospice in any form is designed to give us heart's ease.

On the practical side, both public and private hospice programs must be paid for by private means, insurance, or charitable dollars. In order to have Medicare and Medicaid hospice benefits kick in, the law specifies that, to qualify for hospice, an individual must have a medical prognosis that life expectancy is six months or less if the illness proceeds as usual and also that no treatments that attempt to cure will be administered. It would appear that the prognosis should be the governing factor, but the law has been interpreted by Medicare in terms of its time limit. Despite assertions to the contrary by a former head of Medicare's parent, the Health Care Financing Administration, or HCFA (now known as the Centers for Medicare & Medicaid Services—CMS), a hospice patient who receives Medicare benefits may well become ineligible for future payments if he or she survives for more than six months. Lucette Lagnado, author of "Mercy Living" and *Wall Street Journal* reporter specializing in issues that affect the elderly, has recounted horror stories about exceptions that prove the rule—old people who have been diagnosed as terminal patients because of cancer, heart disease, or galloping combinations of lethal ailments, yet have lived for three or four years, far beyond the legislated span. In these cases, their hospices and their families have been dunned for five- and six-figure sums by the HCFA. Yet, incredible survivors like these comprise a tiny minority. Between 1994 and 1998, most people who entered a hospice program lived for an average of forty-eight days, a little more than a month and a half. That's a very short time, time enough, perhaps, to make an afghan or mount old photographs in an album but not long enough to plant a seed and see it flower or come to fruit. Since then, though sixty days of hospice care creates the greatest benefits for patients and their families, the time has become shorter still: the 2002 report issued by Last Acts gives the median number of days that patients spent under hospice care in 2001 as twenty-two, and it notes that "dying patients commonly have the support of hospice for less than a week." That's no time at all compared to the half-year that seems to be prescribed by Medicare's rules. People whose bodies insist on living past the six-month mark may be discharged from hospice care only to end up in nursing homes. The costs in dollars of hospice care and a nursing home are roughly the same, and Medicare covers them both. There is no comparison, however, in the emotional costs of uprooting someone from home to be cast abruptly into an alien land. The remedy lies with Congress. Meanwhile, the rules are ruthlessly enforced.

Not so strangely, there's a flip side to the business of admission to a hospice. A study issued in 1995—it has a six-barreled name:

The Study to Understand Prognoses and Preferences for Out-
comes and Risks of Treatment, or SUPPORT—notes an optimism,
a pro-life stance in physicians that holds them back from recom-
mending hospice care for patients who are truly in a terminal
state. Most patients in the study died, although their doctors had
predicted that they had a chance for recovery. So, with that hope,
the doctors would not have referred them to hospice. The lesson
is that we who are still hale but are likely one day to be patients
ourselves must arm ourselves and our families with all the information we can possibly obtain.

All hospices face the dilemma of having to discharge seven-
month survivors who are certifiably very sick or to face repayment
of the costs that Medicare has reimbursed. Damned if you do,
damned if you don't. Here, however, compassion may overwhelm
the financial considerations. And some caring physicians, who see
the brutal nonsensicality of the six-month rule, have found a way
around it: if a patient does not expire within that time, then they
will make a new prognosis that only half a year at most is left.
With that, as if it had never been stopped, the clock starts ticking
anew.

Where would hospices be without their volunteers? Volunteers, the sine qua non of any hospice program, perform tasks from
fund-raising to visiting the dying. And funds are always needed.
I go on a fact-finding mission. A friend, Katie Letcher Lyle, has
been intimately involved with the Rockbridge Area Hospice,
headquartered in Lexington, Virginia. The hospice, founded in
1984, typifies the independent, nonprofit model. Katie began her
volunteer association there in 1992 and has since served on its
board. It was started as a strictly volunteer organization but was
federally certified in 1993, nine years after its founding, and now
employs ten people part-time and nine full-time, including social

workers and an executive director. At any given moment, the volunteers number from fifty to seventy and range in age from the twenties into the eighties. The certification, Katie says, drove away some of the volunteers because it entailed abiding by bureaucratic rules that engendered a massive onslaught of paperwork. For them, it seemed that compassion had been willy-nilly swept away by regulatory requirements. Certification, however, had the virtue of making the hospice eligible for Medicare money. But RAH stays faithful to its earliest mission: compassion. It turns down no one who seeks admission. Today, RAH's yearly expenses amount to about $900,000. In fiscal 2002, eighty-seven percent of that came in through Medicare from the Centers for Medicare & Medicaid Services. The remaining dollars must be found in local pocketbooks.

"We have a small population," Katie says. "Having only ten clients drains our resources, but with twenty we're comfortable. It's the difference between a little Medicare and a lot. Just the same, it's tough to raise money in a little rural area." Nonetheless, coming up with funds is an absolute requirement in order to pay for nursing care and pain-relieving drugs. One patient cost RAH nearly $22,000 for morphine before she died, and on the day of her death, United Parcel Service delivered another $2,000 worth, which had to be flushed because of a no-return policy on scheduled drugs. The hospice staff members and doctors who work with them learn by such sympathetic mistakes. Now prescriptions are written for only two or three days' worth of drugs—a sensible practice, for the average stay with RAH is only sixty-three days, with the median stay much shorter, at only twenty-five days. To make up the difference between insurance payments and total costs, Katie and her co-volunteers engage in an exhausting array of fund-raisers. Several years ago, an outdoor breakfast in Katie's brick-walled garden, with testimonials by the survivors of hospice clients, brought in $10,000. Every October, the Hospice Hustle takes place—a four-mile walk on a planned route through Lexington or nearby Buena Vista. Sponsors agree to give prizes to participants and make donations in the name of the walkers. The first week in December brings Light Up a Life, held on Lexington's Hopkins Green and on Magnolia Avenue in Buena Vista. There the names of clients are read out in a ringing roll call; some gifts are made in honor of the living, whose names are also read. I imagine the December chill, the darkness, the candles in hand and the candles of the stars, and, oh, the chanting voices. Eighteen years means a lot of names. On the other hand, Katie has manned information booths at many street fairs and similar celebrations. She says that people will cross the road to avoid walking directly past a booth so intimately connected with death. They do not want to contemplate a donation, much less their own mortality. So far, though, RAH has managed to take on all comers and abide with most of them until their lives end.

Later, I talk in 2000 and again in 2002, with Susan Hogg, RAH's Executive Director. On the first occasion, clad in black pants and a brightly striped shirt, she is a pleasant, slow-voiced woman in her mid-thirties. Her straight dark brown hair gleams, her face lights frequently with smiles. And she is busy. While I sit in her office, which is lined with books, posters, and a large photo of her four-year-old son, the phone rings frequently, volunteers pop in and out, and someone comes to pick up a wheelchair for a patient. When she apologizes for the interruptions, I tell her that there's no need for apology—I'm getting a good view of her usual day. I also have a chance to read a poster-sized Thank You message pinned to one wall: "To everyone at the Rockbridge Area Hospice, From the depths of our beating hearts, we thank each of you for your gentle spirits, your professional expertise, your attentiveness to all our needs."

One of Susan's calls is a chiller, and she quickly contacts the social worker assigned to this case. It seems that a prospective patient is wielding a shotgun. "Don't go in his home alone," Susan tells the social worker. "Not unless someone else is with you." I am impressed. There's no thought of abandoning the patient. It's just that precautions must be taken.

How did she come to this kind of work? Because of a grand-mother who was a resident in a Virginia nursing home. After Susan graduated from college with a B.S. in psychology, she went on to a vocational-technical school where she took courses that qualified her as a CNA. Then she went to work at the nursing home in which her grandmother resided. When her grandmother died, Susan moved to Florida, where she first worked as an activities director in a nursing home and later became a medical secretary at Hospice by the Sea ("actually by Interstate 95," she says). During her five years with the hospice, it grew from thirty patients at a time to one hundred and fifty. "I was miserable at the nursing home," she says. "But I was overjoyed to be part of a quality-of-life hospice."

She was interviewed by RAH in December, 1992, and started work in early 1993.

I ask, "Do you find it hard to work closely with the dying?"

"Everyone will say there's a burn-out factor," she responds. "But no more so than in any other occupation. People who do hospice work are pretty unique to begin with."

How do patients come to hospice? Anyone can start a referral—doctor, family, neighbor, and, indeed, the prospective patient. The referral is completed by a doctor's okay, which amounts to his educated guess that the person being referred has no more than six months of life left and that no curative treatments will be introduced into the person's care. In Susan's sense of things, most of the patients referred are quite rational, not demented. And in her experience, it's the families who are often resistant to hospice. "Our biggest barrier is denial. People don't want to acknowledge dying. Dying is all about loss, and the process involves many losses. Having a strong spiritual faith can mean less of a struggle because those with faith never thought they had control to begin with. But RAH is not a coercive agency. The patient or the patient's designated representative must *want* hospice."

During its years of existence, RAH has served between 600 and 800 patients. Susan's not sure of the number, but it doesn't matter. What counts is the hospice's purpose. She says, "The biggest thing hospice does is education. We are the catalyst for getting others to solve problems. We arm patient and family to make their own choices. If you don't know there's something for nausea, you suffer." If you don't know that there are better and worse ways of departing this world, then you also suffer. RAH and its sisters worldwide provide an anodyne for dying.

On a later visit in 2002, I ask if the hospice ever discharges patients. "Yes," she replies, "but we like to call it graduation. There are such stringent guidelines. Because of Medicare, we live with fiscal fear and must continuously prove that we're within the six-month limit. We're at the smallest end of the hospice scale, with fifteen to twenty-five patients at any one time. So, one patient can make or break the year's budget, and we need an average of eighteen paying patients a day to make ends meet. We reached that goal in 2002." In the same year an impressive 75 percent of RAH's patients were able to die in their own homes, while 20 percent died in nursing homes and only a trifling five percent in the hospital. These figures reverse the usual statistics.

On our first encounter, I learn that there are border raids, with a hospice based in one area expanding its claims to territory well into that of another hospice. The goal: to gain patients whose payments will come to the raider. The solution: to join forces, although doing so may seem a forfeiture of identity that has been painstakingly, compassionately built over decades.

I also ask Susan about the other end of the spectrum: do patients ever ask for help in speeding the dying process? Are there requests for assisted suicide? She nods. "Yes, but the stance of hospice is that when a desire like that is voiced, it's an attention-getting device. We hear not a wish to die but rather discomfort or pain, and we ask what is missing in the patient's quality of life. What can the patient achieve? The social worker and the nurse go through a suicide assessment to determine the seriousness of the demand. When we learn the true reason for such a request, when pain and stress and terror are relieved, there's often a one-hundred-and-eighty degree improvement."

I ask her how she views the concept "quality of life." Is there any such thing as a life without it? She answers quickly, "You don't keep doing what you do without a payoff."

And I present the question most critical to me. "Is human life intrinsically sacred?"

She breathes deeply but does not speak. She glances into the distance, then at the photo of her son. Whatever her response, it will be carefully thought out. Finally, she speaks. "Yes, but that doesn't mean there isn't a good time for death."

To the tune of ringing phones, we've talked for two hours. But when I leave Susan's office, I find that I'm not quite yet able to leave the building. Three volunteers are in RAH's bright and capacious lobby, one standing, one sitting, one behind the desk. All volunteers undergo intensive training, and those who work with patients must complete twenty-four additional hours of training. I sink onto the comfortable sofa and ask all three their motives for volunteering at a hospice. Peter, who is standing, says, "Giving back what life has given to me. I'm much impressed with my fellow volunteers." Ann, behind the desk, says, "It's rewarding to work for a small organization. You feel you're part of a team." The third volunteer is Debbie, a board member of RAH and a registered nurse. In her opinion, "Hospice nursing is the most perfect there is—art and science, the best bedside nursing. More than that, the people affiliated give not one-hundred percent but two-hundred, something you would not find in all institutions."

I think that when my own life finds time for another activity—and it will—I'd like to be a hospice volunteer.

HOSPICE HAS touched me twice, once with my mother, then in 2002, during the last days of my husband, the Chief. A hospice nurse, who comes after dark to take us on board when I've realized that I can no longer give him all the care—the transfers, the bathing—that he needs, gives me a booklet on that first night. It is *Gone from My Sight: The Dying Experience* by Barbara Karnes, a registered nurse and former hospice director. And it lists the signs that indicate the approach of death. They are many and appear en masse or only partially, depending on the person who is dying, for each death is a unique event. A month or so beforehand, there may be a withdrawal, a closing into self, along with a loss of interest in food and an increase in sleep. One to two weeks beforehand, the signs may consist of disorientation and talking with the dead; blood pressure may decrease, body temperature may become noticeably hot or cold, and the skin may take on a pale or bluish tinge. Days or hours before death, these signs will intensify and be accompanied by restlessness, a decreased urine output, and skin that's become blotchy or purplish. Without hospice, I would not have known these things.

CAROL, the hospice nurse calls. "Your mother's been with us now for four months, and she's really much better. Best if she leaves hospice at this point, so that if she needs it later, it will still be available."

And she is better. We take her out of the hospice program. Not long after the antibiotics and antihistamines are withdrawn from her daily regimen, she opens her eyes and hungrily opens her mouth. Since then, she has been eating with a gargantuan appetite and struggling to rise from her recliner. She's full of get-up-and-go. But where would she go? Where can she?

The Quality of Life

O Rose, thou art sick!
The invisible worm
That flies in the night
In the howling storm

Has found out thy bed
Of crimson joy:
And his dark secret love
Does thy life destroy.

—William Blake, "The Sick Rose"

IT TAKES ONLY a few weeks for Sarah to regress. She does not shut her eyes and clench her teeth this time. Instead, she becomes like an infant, unable to comprehend the basic elements of the world around her—shelter, clothing, food. Instinct tells her that she must eat, and goodness knows that she tries to feed herself, though she can no longer distinguish what is edible from what is not. Her placemat, her napkin, her bib, the cuff of her sweater, the hem of a caregiver's T-shirt—all are variously grasped and stuffed into her mouth. At other times, she tries to rise from her wheelchair or her recliner. For the last two years she has been so incapacitated that she cannot give the caregivers any assistance when they move her from bed to wheelchair, wheelchair to recliner. Rosa says that when Sarah is lifted, she is as floppy as a rag doll. Wearing back supports, the caregivers lift her and waltz her one tiny step at a time from one place to the next. But though her legs don't work, her arms do, and her upper body strength is amazing. Pushing up and forward, she attempts to thrust herself out of the chair, a worrisome act, for if she were to succeed—and she easily could do so—she would fall and, likely, an old, osteoporotic bone would snap. The caregivers are cagey, not admitting anything, but I know that when none of the family is present, they have restrained her, they have kept her in the wheelchair or recliner with wide straps. But if that's the best way that they can keep her from hurting herself and the only way that they are free to attend to other household duties, like laundry and preparing meals, so be it. I can only commend their attentiveness and deep regard for Sarah. Once, before she entered hospice care, she seemed to be mostly contented and cheerful. Now, she weeps frequently, face red and swollen, tears coursing down her cheeks.

What can we do? Her world has shrunk to bedroom, bath, den, and diningroom table, with occasional forays to the doctor or the dentist. Nor is she aware that Muffin, her little white poodle, aged seventeen and suffering from congestive heart failure, was taken to the vet and put to sleep. People no longer come to see her, for she cannot converse, nor, often, can she understand what is being said. Her vocabulary is restricted to "Good," and "Yes," and occasionally, "No," though she has spells of babbling like someone speaking in tongues. Does she know what she is saying, even if no one else can interpret her scatter-shot glossolalia? Impossible to tell. Nor does she always recognize familiar faces. When I see her these days, she often scowls and shakes her head in puzzlement. Our days of story-reading stopped not long before hospice care began, for her comprehension had become erratic. I tell her my name, but it either doesn't register or she thinks that I am her mother. And, sensing that something is wrong, she becomes obviously upset. I stay, nonetheless, and deliver a monologue or talk with the caregiver on duty. The sound of human beings speaking softly seems to have an effect as soothing as a lullaby. Sometimes, however, she is visited by a talkative family member of whom she is not fond, a family member caught in deep denial of the fact that Sarah's chances for recovery are nonexistent. The result: Sarah delivers a strong nonverbal message by putting on the face that led to her months with hospice—eyes tightly shut, mouth closed. It is a face that says plainly, belligerently, "Leave me alone. Go away."

But she doesn't know where she is. Her needs are tended to with diligence and never-failing respect, but I come to wonder if she might not be a good candidate for a nursing home. Surely, there are places that can care for her as gently, as thoroughly as she's cared for in the house she no longer recognizes as her own and, yes, at far less expense. To maintain round-the-clock caregivers on a private basis costs in the high five figures every year. On top of that come the ordinary household expenses for food, heat, electricity, water, taxes, insurance, repairs, cable television (which is used as a babysitter), and all the other quotidian luxuries and necessities. I ask my brothers and sisters what they think about the possibility of moving her to a facility with skilled care. Three meet the notion with reluctance but willingness at least to explore it; one accuses me of ranking costs as a criterion higher than the best care for our mother. Ironically, that one is the child to whom she gave a mortgage, which has not been repaid by one jot or tittle. That issue is unresolved and looms, therefore, a mighty factor in the accusation. Nonetheless, Joe and I make an appointment to visit a nursing home that has been recommended by our attorney as a place of excellent care and fine cheer. It is owned and run by Mennonites recently returned from missionary work in Central America. And when we visit in early December, three years after Sarah's second stroke, we see the reasons that the facility comes with high recommendations. The patients in the large dayroom occupy recliners rather than wheelchairs, and many are wide awake and conversing. No stupefying drugs that deaden restlessness seem to be used here, nor do we see any sign of restraints. If any patients here are strapped down to keep them from roaming or falling, it is not done in the nursing home's public places. Sunlight streams through picture windows that frame a view of the Blue Ridge. The patients are clean and neatly dressed, the tables and floors gleam, nor do we catch a single whiff of stale urine or diseased flesh. Joe visits with some of the old ladies while I talk with the proprietors. When I ask if my mother's living will and DNR will be respected, they give me full assurances. I fill out an application and write a check for a deposit. Though they have no opening at present for another patient, they expect to add eight rooms to the facility within the next few months. A staff nurse, however, will come to visit Sarah and assess her needs and personality so that when a room becomes available—and should she pass the assessment—she may be moved right in.

The nurse, a pleasant blonde woman wearing casual clothes, comes in mid-February. I have not told the caregivers that a nurse was coming but rather that a friend of mine would be here with me that day. Deviousness is excusable, I think, because it is not certain that Sarah will be moved out of her own home. More than that, at this point, Rosa and the other two caregivers do not need to start fretting about their jobs. Not knowing what will happen, or when, I want them to stay confident that all's well in their world. Sarah does not need distracted people in her circumscribed life. The interview goes well. Sarah is cheerful, enjoying the company, and she finds a few words to respond to the nurse's questions. "Do you have grandchildren?" the nurse asks. Sarah nods and says, "Yes." "How many?" Sarah smiles sweetly and uses her little girl voice to say, "I don't know." I mourn for her. There is much that she does not know; the time, the day, the season of the year; the names of foods; the names of friends. Before the nurse leaves, we sit in the kitchen and talk briefly. Sarah has qualified for admission; all that's needed is an opening.

We wait for word from the nursing home. We hear nothing. I call to learn when there might be an opening. Construction of the new facility has been delayed. I ask that the deposit be returned. My husband and I leave for North Carolina, where we spend the warmer months, and the possibility of sending Sarah to a nursing home recedes in my mind.

Meanwhile, she catches a cold. It segues into pneumonia, and she comes within a cat's whisker of dying. Breathing stertorously, phlegm gurgling loudly, she lies slumped in her recliner. Back north for a visit, I see and hear these things—and find myself praying that she will die, for her life holds no joy. Except for the stubborn beating of her heart and the flow of air into and out of her lungs, she is totally dependent on other people for everything. The caregivers bathe and dress her, feed her, and take her for occasional wheelchair rides on warm, sunny days. They administer Dilantin and other medications. They make copious notes of all that happens during a day—the menus for meals, the length of her naps, the names of people who drop by with food or flowers, the kinds and ounces of fluids that she is persuaded to drink, the quantity of urine emptied from her Foley bag. They also pay special attention to her skin; one of their triumphs is that she has never had a single bedsore. Then, because Sarah has lost the power to defecate, every third day, Rosa conducts what she calls the "bowel program," the administration of enemas so that fecal material may be loosened and removed. And when she becomes critically ill with pneumonia, the caregivers somehow manage to fill her with antibiotics, and she recovers. For what?

Mindless and grasping, flesh hangs on for not-so-dear life. No matter that reason is gone, and purpose, too, the body insists with brute force on staying alive. In this debacle, my mother is like an empty fortress: the building remains, but all the defenders have fled. Her body lives but no longer houses a person. I mourn for her. And I think she knows in spirit, though not in mind, the turn that her life has taken. Once fine and productive, a joy to herself and others, the quality of her life has deteriorated to a state of wretched helplessness. Her sadness and tears attest to that.

QUALITY OF LIFE—I find that some people regard the idea as a criterion wholly without merit for appraising existence. It raises hackles because of its subjectivity. How is it possible for anyone else to determine the worth of someone's life? Talking with friends and with professional health-care providers, I go in search of enlightenment. Cut-and-dried answers may not exist, but surely, somewhere in the wilderness, guidelines will be found. In the end, I do find objective criteria, and from a source that at first astonishes me but soon seems inevitable: Abdulaziz Sachedina, the gentle and devout Muslim bioethicist with whom I talked at the University of Virginia.

My own physician offers generalities. "It's personal," he says. "For some, quality of life is defined as just existing and being aware of loved ones regardless of personal suffering. Then, I have patients who are physically active. If they were deprived, they'd lose quality." One of his tasks, then, is to act according to the views of each patient, which may range from longevity at all costs to a wish not to be kept alive by artificial means. In the process, he must keep his own views to himself lest the patient be unduly influenced by the authority almost automatically possessed by an experienced doctor (and some who may not be experienced but have the diploma attesting to their formal education framed and prominently displayed on an office wall). I have given him a copy of my DPA and stated my wishes directly. They shall, I am sure, be honored.

I find a more pointed view in the syndicated newspaper column of Dr. Peter Gott. A reader asks, "How on earth can we justify keeping the elderly alive year after year—up to 110 or 120 in a few decades, if we believe the experts—when the quality of their lives will be so hideously compromised, even in the face of future medical advances?" The good doctor responds with a question of his own: "Is charming and frail aunt Ella going to be better off living to 110, using heroic medical therapy, if she is bed-ridden, doesn't know she is on planet Earth, and is hopelessly incontinent?"

He goes on to state his own wishes: "Longevity may be a great goal, but it has to be accompanied by an equally important end-game, called quality of life." He would not become a burden to his family, nor would he "squander" his savings to be kept alive because a doctor feels bound to save life and stave off death or because someone else has issues that cannot be resolved if he should die. It would be fine to live as long as Methuselah if—and it's a large if—we remain aware of the things around us and can make decisions for ourselves. Otherwise, he prays that "we will be cared for by sensitive physicians who consider helpless, irreconcilable, inhuman dependency a far greater enemy than death." He triggers an important question: Are there conditions to which a human being may be subject that are worse than death? And he answers loud and clear: Yes.

Seeking further definitions and opinions from people engaged in the care of those who are sick and dying, I find that they are ready and willing, even eager, to talk about the issues. "You really have to know somebody well to know what quality of life means." So Steve Henderson tells me. A psychologist whose practice focuses on people who are dying, he trained with Elisabeth Kübler-Ross, deservedly famous for her investigations into the stages of life's last journey, and has served over the years on her advisory board. On several occasions, he helped lead her workshops on "Life, Death and Transition." The five stages that she was the first to identify— denial and isolation, anger, bargaining, depression, acceptance— have since been joined by two more, finishing old business, in which life is reviewed and troubling issues resolved, and transcendence, or a psychospiritual transformation that marries the dying individual to the universal. The first five are experienced not only by the dying but also by the living, who also and all too often refuse to face truth and rage at the dying of someone else's light. The last two are supposedly available only to someone nearing death. But Steve has opinions to the contrary, which will be mentioned shortly.

Steve and I meet in a restaurant that used to be the lobby of the town's train station. As we dine, a freight train rumbles massively by, creating vibrations that tickle our feet. Steve is sixty years old, with white beard, white hair, and shaggy white brows. I learn that he's a musician and folk-art collector as well as a psychologist. His voice brims over with a contagious energy. Steve himself is something of a miracle, the survivor of not one but two kidney transplants. The first one came from his father in 1966, when Steve was only twenty-four years old, and the second from his brother in 1987. When he first became ill, no one, including the physicians, talked with him about dying. He struggled for a while to face the severity of his disorder, read everything about renal disease that he could get his hands on, and came at last to a point at which he could think about death and dying in relation to himself. And he had to get there alone. He says, "The freedom I experienced is that you can live in the present because you don't have to worry about the future, about security. Now, though, I have to worry about old age and retirement. But somehow in my own mind, it didn't seem right that I was okay with dying. Seemed like it was un-American."

I think of a dictum of the Buddha: "Those who decide 'I will die' stop being afraid." And I respond that it may well be un-American not to fight for survival, even against monumental odds. Indeed, many people believe that the right thing to do is not only to resist the grim reaper and fight to the very end but also to do it at home. These days, however, more Americans die in hospitals or nursing facilities than in their homes, a fact that puts death out of sight. Steve, who has traveled widely in Central America, says that he has found Mexicans much more comfortable in dealing with death, humanizing it and making it part of everyday life. "And," he adds, "for most of the Asian societies, death is a part of growth and enlightenment. Do you suppose that resisting the idea of death is peculiarly Christian? If you look at the basic tenets of the Christian church, it's built around a person dying. But we are very death-denying. We get from Palm Sunday to the Resurrection as quickly as we possibly can." He punctuates this thought with a laugh. "There's something about our denial that we know how to die; there's talk about the drive for survival. But we *do* know how to die if we open ourselves to that." His words are totally credible, for he is a man who has faced his own death intimately not once but twice.

He speaks, too, of the final stages of dying—the resolution of old business and transcendence. He thinks they're not restricted to those on the verge of death. "It seems to me," he says, "that one of the gifts the dying give all of us who are willing to be with them is the knowledge that dealing with unfinished business at any stage of our life is important and liberating. It's even one of the steps of the AA program. The dying and the sense of our own mortality teach us the importance of telling people we love them and that they made a difference in our lives. They teach us to mend fences and to reach out to those who have been important to us. I also believe that by facing our own mortality, we can achieve at least some transformation."

Asserting that it's often necessary for people to fight for the right to die, he tells of a member of his extended family who recently died of an advanced lung cancer, the kind that works its ravages very quickly. "He very clearly made the decision right from the beginning that he didn't want any chemotherapy or any treatment. He wanted palliative care. He wasn't afraid; he was going to go ahead and die. But some of the medical people just ran over him like a steamroller. Now, they didn't succeed. This is a man who has been schizophrenic all his life, but he still had the strength to hang in there. The doctors kept making referral after referral, assuming that he wanted treatment, that there'd be no side effects, all sorts of hogwash. The worst was that his psychiatrist called the hospital shocked that his patient wouldn't fight to the very end. Psychiatrists like that should have their license taken away. The fact is that there are a lot of people out there who are deniers. Denial must really run deep in our society. Think of all the people who die without wills."

I ask Steve for his views on how best to care for someone who is old and demented. He allows that care is made more complicated because they cannot participate. One of the problems is that people put off addressing end-of-life issues until it is too late. "When I'm with people who are demented, I try to listen really carefully to their expressions and body movements and whatever else it is that I can listen to in order to figure out what's going on. Sometimes there are precious few clues. It's really important that families talk about the issues of death and dying ahead of time."

When it comes to defining the term "quality of life," he tells of an exercise done in groups. Each participant is asked to name ten things without which individual identity would disappear. How many might you have taken away and still be you? How would you be different without one of the ten? Without a second one? Steve says, "People differ in their lists. If you reach a point that you're no longer you, that's the point at which you might choose to die. Some people can't give up anything." Quality of life, then, depends partly on your ability to adapt to changes and loss.

Before we part, he suggests that I talk with Lynn Coyner, a nurse who specializes in end-of-life issues. I call right away to arrange a meeting. Now in her early fifties, Lynn began her career as a registered nurse thirty-three years ago, earned an undergraduate degree in thanatology—the study of death—and a master's degree in nursing, and received a fellowship to study ethics at the University of Virginia. Today, she not only serves on the ethics committee of a regional hospital but also acts as its director of services that range from birth to death—Obstetrics,

Oncology, Emergency, Progressive Care, and Intensive Care. Early one July morning, we meet at her forty-acre farm, where she and a friend raise forty-plus alpacas for their wool. Her clothing, white and blue, matches the summer sky. Her hair is brown with a touch of red; her face full and graced with a welcoming smile. Inviting me to sit at an outdoor table, she serves coffee and fruit—red raspberries, blackberries—that she picked not long before I arrived. The alpacas—black, white, chocolate brown, silvery gray, caramel—have moseyed from the barn into an outdoor enclosure and eye us curiously. She points to several and names them, "Phoebe, Jet, Houdini." A song-sparrow, perched high in a near-by juniper, carols throughout our talk.

The quality-of-life concept has long figured in Lynn's think-ing. "Quality of life," she says, "is a real issue for me because it's a personal thing. It's hard for people who are caring for other people not to impose their own opinions and emotions into it. I learned that with dialysis patients or chronically ill people. You'd hear people say, 'I'd never go on dialysis, never. Three times a week, four or five hours a day—it would just not be worth living.' But people with chronic disease have such an insidious process that they learn to adapt to their disability. So, by the time they get to the point of needing dialysis or other rehabilitative therapy, they've accommodated to what their quality of life is at the time." I am reminded of Steve Henderson's exercise of ten items without which you would not be you. Lynn says that she has often seen a patient's perspective change during the course of an illness. Some-one who has resisted dialysis at first, for example, comes to find that it is a viable option because it allows life not only to continue but also to include many activities. They may not be activities pur-sued before the onset of illness, but, like former interests, they provide a host of benefits—pleasure, physical exercise, mental stimulation. There is the joy, too, of finding out that an old dog can indeed learn new tricks. Adaptation is part of the aging process. "Some people," Lynn says, "do it quicker than others because of illness. The quality of life changes depending on what's wrong with you." And she mentions Christopher Reeves, once Superman in the movies, now a quadriplegic who devotes his still fierce energies to advocacy for the disabled. His quality of life has undergone an enormous transformation, but he has indeed adapted, despite ongoing periods of depression, to a life greatly, grievously altered by an untoward accident.

Some people, however, do not or cannot adapt. Lynn tells the story of her father, who died only two weeks before she and I meet to talk. Eighty-five years old and frail, living in a nursing home, he would not sign an advance medical directive, for he carried the hope that somehow he would come to feel better. "My mother had myeloplastic syndrome, and she ended up converting to acute leukemia. She was adamant about, 'I do not want to be resuscitated if I'm going to end up living on machines.' So she had no problem with that at all. But Dad wasn't willing to do that. He always had a lot of spark." He could not, however, adapt his interests, his way of life to his increasing frailty and failing health. When Lynn would ask him what he wanted to do, he'd say, "I want to play golf." But given the fact that he was no longer able to play the game, Lynn would suggest using golf video games or watching television. It soon became clear to her that if he could not do just as he used to do, he was going to do nothing more than sit in a chair.

The lack of an advance medical directive might have caused an unfortunate attempt at resuscitation. When the nursing home telephoned Lynn and her sister, who lives nearby, to say that he had gone precipitously downhill, was not responsive, and would soon be transported to the hospital by the rescue squad, she called the squad, begging them not to do CPR. But the rescue squad said that, without a DNR, they were obligated to keep life going by any means necessary. But Lynn has an access to the hospital staff that most people don't have. She called the emergency department and asked to speak with an ER doctor. "I asked, 'Can you please, please, please call the rescue squad and tell them not to do CPR?' They can do that with an order from a physician. I just could not imagine them beating on my daddy as old and frail as he was." As it happened, her father had died by the time that the rescue squad arrived.

The friend who owns eight of the alpacas arrives, fretting. One of her babies has lost its mother but refuses to nurse from a bottle. Later, Lynn and I shall see the orphan sneaking milk from another mother. And it *is* a sneaky operation, for the mother would ordinarily refuse to nurse a baby other than her own. But her baby is good-sized, and the little one can hide in the shadow of the slightly larger animal to butt and suck at the mother's second teat. To help out with this unsuspected double duty, the mother will be given extra feed.

I ask Lynn about her thoughts on the sanctity of life, which is sometimes set in opposition to the concept of its quality. She takes a sip of coffee. "I think the sanctity of life is extremely important," she says slowly, thoughtfully. "But I also think we have to be realistic. When people get to the point that there's no purposeful life left, that can be very hard to deal with. It's very hard to deal with families because some families, being religious, will talk about how it's God's will and God decides. Then I have to look at the situation and say to myself that if God has decided, the machines wouldn't be hooked up, and the patient would already be dead. It's hard in many respects to get families to understand that anything we would do at this point would be futile. We're not prolonging life. All we're doing is prolonging death. I truly believe in the sanctity of life, but I think that when you get to the point of not having a purposeful existence, it's time to let go."

I ask if she believes that human life has more sanctity than that of alpacas, and she replies, "No, I think everything is equal in that respect. As the director of OB now, I never cease to be amazed. I just want to hold my breath till the babies come out and they're breathing. I've seen it done hundreds of times, and it's still amazing. And delivering the baby alpacas—these little things come out looking like spiders with all those long legs, and within an hour they're struggling to get up, they're moving, they're trying to nurse. I've delivered quite a few of them." She glances happily at the curious mob in the outdoor enclosure. "I like to sit out here and look around and be amazed."

She returns to the difficulty of understanding that there comes to everyone a time to die. "I think that the futility issue is so hard for a lot of people because some families just want life by any means, any measure, any cost." When I add that you can't come to terms with sorrow or find closure when someone is kept artificially, unnaturally alive, she says, "Much of that has to do with guilt. I see that all the time. People want that family member to stay alive because they never did anything for him, and if he stays alive, they don't have to deal with the fact of death and the feeling that they didn't do as they were supposed to do. We see that quite a lot in health care. You'll get family members who come in—one was the caretaker and the other did nothing. They will have differences of opinion. The caretaker says, 'Mother would never have wanted to live like this. She's had a good quality of life till now.' And the other one says, 'Oh, we need to do everything to keep her alive.'"

She illustrates her point with the story of an ethics consultation. The patient was an older woman who lived in a nursing home and had suffered a stroke, whereupon, very ill, she was taken to the hospital. She was not responsive and could not communicate; the prognosis for recovery was poor. How best to treat her? Her sons fell into a dispute. One, who had acted on occasion as her caretaker, wanted everything possible to be done—ventilator, intubation, the works. He said that before the stroke his mother had been up, walking around the nursing home and otherwise doing very well indeed. The other son, who lived in another state, advocated keeping her comfortable while events took a natural course. Argument had overwhelmed the decision-making process. An ethics mediation session was held at the hospital. One of the difficulties was apparent from the outset: The woman had made a durable health care power of attorney in which she named not one son as her agent with the other as his successor but rather both were made co-agents from the start. Speaking slowly and deliberately, emphasizing each word, Lynn says, *"Co-power of attorney for health care—nobody should ever do this.* Tell people that." The ethics consultation took nearly three hours. Lynn and a colleague refrained from joining in the discussion; their role was to listen and to ask questions that would stimulate progress. Lynn says, "This is the question we asked most: 'Is this what your mother would have wanted? Make your decisions on what she would want, not what you want. It's what your mother would have chosen to have happen.' " The discussion became heated at times, with anger, bellicosity, aggression, and defensiveness all making an entrance. Lynn describes one brother as a man responding to emotion, while the other was far calmer and more thoughtful. At last, a compromise was achieved. The two decided that their mother would have a feeding tube, but that if there was no improvement within a time determined by her physician, it would be removed and she would be allowed to die. "We felt very successful with that one," Lynn says. "You do feel good about having a family come together."

We discuss communications then. The great problem that Lynn encounters in ethics consultations is that people have not discussed their wishes with family members or their doctors. The difficulty is compounded when families, stressed to the hilt as they try to deal with dying, have trouble understanding not only the technical explanations but also the emotion-laden assessments given by health-care professionals—the doctor who doesn't want to discuss death, the nurse who knows just what should be done. Often there's no one in control. But an ethics committee brings all the forces together so that an unresolved issue may be examined from all sides.

I ask Lynn if she thinks that economics plays a role in the decisions that families make. She replies, "Not enough. You see families who are totally destroyed financially. Perhaps one family member wants everything done, but it's really futile care. I think we need to talk about money a whole lot more because most of the dollars that are spent in health-care are spent at the end of life. I think you have to go back to what is purposeful and real. They say it's so hard to make a decision about who could live and who could die. But we do it every day. Families and doctors and nurses together make decisions whether to continue treatment or stop it. We just don't do it formally." She hopes that there will eventually be well-regulated places, in-patient hospices, to which people who no longer wish to live may go.

As our conversation winds down, Lynn tells me a story that illustrates the summoning of the living by the dead. She says, "My grandmother talked to several people in the last two weeks before she died. I remember sitting with her in the afternoon, and she told me, 'Lynn, I've just seen all these people. It was wonderful. I saw Aunt Daisy, and I've seen Mary Elizabeth'—her daughter— 'and they were all standing in a group beckoning me to come.' My grandmother went through a whole litany of people who were dead. Then, one day, she called me at work and said, 'Lynn, I think I'm dying.' So I jumped in the car and went running over there. She was lying on the sofa in the family room, and she looked so peaceful and so sweet. I asked her if she was all right. She said, 'I am. After I called you, Doctor came.' That was what she called her husband, who had been a physician. 'He's sitting right here with me,' she said, 'and I've felt fine since then.' I told her that I'd just sit there with both of them. It was wonderful."

The song sparrow in the evergreen tree is still caroling. I hear it as we go to the barn to visit the alpacas. They are skittish with a stranger in their midst but nonetheless cluster around at what they must regard as a safe distance. Lynn catches one of the babies. I put my palm on the little animal's fur—it is dense, cinnamon brown, and soft as plush.

Most of us do not have Lynn's training and experience. We slog through a pathless wilderness or venture onto a sea marked, like those on old mariners' maps, *Hic dracones*—here be serpents. Bumbling, misjudging, occasionally (if unwittingly) doing the right thing, we learn as we go.

A friend introduces me by mail to Tess, an ardent gardener and golfer, despite total replacements for both of her knees. She cared for her parents, both in their eighties, for seven years until her mother died and then for three and a half more years while her father lingered on. Her story involves classic elements—naiveté and sheer ignorance; delay in responding to need; lack of communication between Tess and her parents, John and Martha, and between Tess and her sister, Judy; dementia in both old people; and the stress placed upon the caregiver.

Her father, a retired professor, suffered a stroke in 1978, but it had become evident before that event that both old people needed help with the tasks of daily life. Tess says, "It was easy to delay making changes till it became glaringly obvious that things couldn't continue as they were." Alternating lifelong between spells of inactivity and bursts of activity, her mother had a history of what would now be diagnosed as bipolar disorder. In a manic state, she would ride her bicycle on campus wearing a halter top and culottes—not a wise move at the time—and then feel hurt almost to the point of paranoia because she did not receive the regard from faculty wives that she thought she deserved. Tess's father, faced with Hobson's choice, had decided to live with Martha's problems instead of allowing her to continue psychiatric treatments that he found exceedingly difficult to accept.

When it became evident that Tess's parents needed assistance, she assumed a caregiver's role by default, for her sister lived several states away. She opted for home care during the first seven years and every Sunday made a hundred-and-forty-mile round-trip to check on her parents' needs and well-being. The first order of business was to find someone who would come into her parents' home and do the quotidian chores, like meal preparation and light cleaning. Anxious to find help, Tess made the mistake of taking on someone recommended as "a good Christian woman" without checking her references. This supposedly principled woman proceeded to steal small items and forge checks. Dismissing the woman proved easier, however, than dealing with the bank, which Tess felt had been negligent, and working with the police, who could do very little to achieve justice without putting her parents—"these two demented old people"—on the witness stand. This experience led to hiring insured, bonded help through an agency. And so life continued for the next seven years, when it became evident that both Martha and John, whose health was in decline, would be better cared for in a nursing facility located close to Tess's own home. Her mother's behavior did not change so much as her father's, but Tess says, "I learned to expect extremes from her, such as staying up at night, writing letters and being busy, busy, then sleeping excessively, failing to change clothes or bathe, and failing to experience pleasure in anything. As for her father, his judgment became impaired to the point that it was no longer safe for him to drive. The first step was to take away the car keys, and the next, to remove the battery. The car was finally sold. Once, Tess drove him to a reunion with his four surviving brothers and sisters at the home of a cousin who lived in an adjoining state, an occasion that she expected him to relish, but on return he accused her of being a bad person. Why? Because she had missed a highway exit on the way home (she says that the lapse caused little inconvenience). Then, in his book, she was also a bad mother because one of her teen-aged sons had been obliged to go to summer school to take a civics class. "It was hard to realize," she says, "that this was the same person who had been so gentle and fair for most of the time I had known him."

Tess's next task was convincing her sister Judy, along with Judy's family, that the move to a nursing home was truly necessary. "I was incensed," Tess recalls, "when my sister sent me a letter listing a series of reasons that our father shouldn't be put in a nursing facility. This came after I had related to her a recent experience in which he'd become physically violent toward me." The move to a nearby nursing home involved time and red tape but was finally accomplished in September, 1985. Tess's husband, whom she describes as "in this with me all the way," had already been named in her parents' will as executor of their estates, but neither parent had ever discussed with Tess, or with anyone, their wishes should they become incapacitated. Because they had made neither a living will nor a DPA, Tess went to court in order to be appointed their legal guardian. She then tackled the job of dismantling her parents' household—and taking every precaution while doing it. Appraisers were hired, and nothing was distributed to grandchildren until every last item had been accounted for.

After the move, Martha fell, broke a hip, and began a precipitous slide downhill. Tess opted not to take heroic measures, but was under such stress when faced with the issue that she found herself doing activities, like laundry and mowing the grass, that required no decision-making. "Mother showed increased signs of dementia," Tess says, "and wasn't eating or drinking sufficient amounts to survive. I spent lots of time trying to feed her at the nursing facility. I wanted to make my sister aware of her condition. So that she wouldn't be surprised by a phone call telling her that Mother had died, I described my failure to get significant amounts of food and liquids into her. Judy's solution to the problem was to send a fancy box of chocolates, which arrived two days before Mother died. My sister couldn't find the time to visit Mother before she died, but she was able to spend four or five days doing Scottish dances and pageantry with a group that celebrates clan history. Her family was at that time concerned about her drinking. I got the feeling that reality, for Judy, was whatever she chose to believe it was."

Martha died in November, 1985, but John lived for three-and-a-half more years and adapted so well to living in the nursing home that when he was taken to Tess's house or on other outings, he was eager to return to his own place. He had begun to experience problems in walking alone, and in February, 1989, he fell and fractured a hip. Tess says, "He was ready to die by late March, but I felt he was being kept alive by overzealous health-care people until late April. I finally ordered them to quit prodding and poking at him unless they were making him comfortable."

She thinks that old people, rational or not, should be made as comfortable as possible. "There needs to be a balance," she says, "between providing high-tech devices and good personal care. I found it upsetting that my father was given a high-tech air bed to safeguard his fragile skin from breaking down, yet there never seemed to be enough caring people around who could take the time and effort to encourage him to drink water on a regular schedule." The problem illustrates the need for nursing homes to be able to pay for caring, reliable, trained, and intelligent employees—a tall order. And if nursing homes increase fees to afford such help, their patients are the ones who pay.

Tess talks about her own life during those years. She experienced frustration at having to miss every Sunday with her husband and children for seven years. She felt helpless, too, though she had no choice other than to do as she did, and this at a time when her children had grown old enough so that, in different circumstances, she would have had the freedom to pursue her own interests. She was angry, too, not only at her parents' plight but also at her sister. She found it hard to do all that needed to be done and at the same time be forced to plead her case over and again to convince family members that certain measures—the sale of the car, the nursing home—were necessary. I ask her if she found rewards in her caregiving. She quotes what her Navy son said after having made it successfully through survival training before going overseas: "I'm glad it's behind me. I'm proud to have gotten through it. I hope I never have to do anything like it again."

Yet, caring for her aged parents changed Tess's life and that of her husband in positive ways. They found it easy to talk about end-of-life issues. Both made living wills that name a health-care representative and are on file with their primary-care physicians. Very soon after Tess's father died, they took out long-term-care insurance—and were still young enough then to qualify for reasonable premiums. (If they were to apply today, the premiums would be exorbitant because costs are based on the age at which the policies are bought. The better companies offering long-term-care policies tend not to raise premiums as time goes by.) Tess and her husband, after looking into the cost of funerals, have pre-planned and set up a trust to pay for them. And Tess describes the greatest gift of her caregiving experience: "I value the time I have left at this stage of my life. I refuse to feel guilty when I decide not to spend any of that time with people who make me crazy."

We talk about the meaning of the phrase "quality of life." Tess's view is that an optimal quality is one in which your responses to your circumstance, in sickness and in health, are positive. Longevity for longevity's sake is not part of her equation. And when it comes to the sanctity of life, she echoes many of the others with whom I've talked. "I don't think life is sacred," she says. "But I'm sure it is miraculous and should be treated with wisdom and respect." She knows that wisdom and respect may be interpreted in different ways and cites a horrid example: humane treatment for animals is mandatory in her way of thinking, but she disagrees vigorously with the people she calls "animal-rights terrorists," who do violence in the name of their cause. Terrorism—an eminently suitable word for lack of wisdom and respect, and one that may be applied to many events, from the callous treatment of some old people to bombing abortion clinics and flying jet aircraft into the World Trade Center and the Pentagon.

To give care to someone who is dying is to be provided with a rich resource for your own life. Tess has taken full advantage of it, becoming confident and comfortable with making preparations for her own final years. Another woman, a friend who spent a long three years serving as the care manager for her increasingly irrational mother, says that the ordeal has made her aware of the burdens from which she would spare her children.

On the other hand, Nancy, who took her mother, Ruth, out of a nursing facility and brought her home to die, has not taken most of the practical steps that caregiving suggests. Though she has a will that distributes her effects, she has not made a living will or a DPA. And her age, over seventy, puts her out of the ballpark for affordable long-term-care premiums. She says, "I told my kids that they're in charge. If I run out of money or sense, they'll just have to take over." She has, however, put her wishes, with occasional updates, into writing and given them to her daughters. But she has gained intangible benefits of the highest order. Before her mother died, Nancy had lost her only son. "What caring for my mother *did* was to extend the attitude that came after my son died: That this is, as far as I know or believe, the only life I'm going to have. Use it well. Don't put off telling people how you feel about them. Eschew game-playing. Take chances. Try to die with no regrets about things not done." She speaks, as a survivor, of now being able to take risks and exercise passions. Her sentiments are not uncommon in survivors everywhere, from people, like Nancy, who suffer mounting losses one at a time to people who live in the face of earthquakes, epidemic disease, and terror.

QUALITY OF LIFE has become a hugely important issue because medical technology has so successfully extended life, often at the expense of living well, that many people suffer a condition that has been called "chronic dying." Just as humankind stood biological destiny on its head when we climbed out of the hunting-gathering niche for which we were designed and began to domesticate animals and crops, so we are controverting biology by being able to alter the natural selection process that has, until very recently, governed the course of our aging. As the authors of an article in the *Scientific American* on human aging have put it:

> The dilemma we face as a society is that medical
> ethics oblige physicians and researchers to pursue
> new technologies and therapeutic interventions in
> efforts to postpone death. Yet that campaign will
> inadvertently accelerate the aging of the population.
> Without a parallel effort to improve the quality of
> life, it may also extend the frequency and duration
> of frailty and disability at older ages.

There is a rule of thumb, a clear lesson, to be drawn here: If intervention can make life better for someone who is dying by restoring a modicum of purpose, health, and pleasure to that person, then it is called for, but if the postponement of death brings no benefits and prolongs suffering, then it is time for us who live to let that person go. People with disabilities—the lame and halt, the blind and deaf, those waiting for transplants, and those eroded by long-term incurable illnesses like multiple sclerosis or diabetes—have expressed grave reservations, however, about the possibilities that someone other than themselves will assess their quality of life and find it abysmally wanting. For several reasons, I think that their fear is largely misplaced. First, the emphasis in health-care lies firmly on the side of maintaining life. Second, patient autonomy has recently become a primary consideration; if you are able to express your wishes, then they are to be heeded. No less than an act of Congress has so decreed—the Patient Self-Determination Act (PSDA), passed in 1991. It stipulates that any hospital receiving federal funds is obliged to tell patients and their families about the legal status of advance medical directives—that they are to be honored absolutely—and to let us know that by signing such a directive we can indeed determine the course of care in our final days. Even before Congress enacted the PSDA, we have had the right to determine our treatment, though we likely did not know that we could do so. As Marilyn Webb, author of *The Good Death,* a fine book on the American search for a death that is peaceful and free of pain, has put it:

> It is not widely understood that patients who are
> conscious and mentally competent have long had
> the right to decide on their own medical treatment,
> that court cases and common law have all supported
> a patient's right to make his or her own medical
> decisions, even if others disagree with those deci-
> sions, and even if those decisions might ultimately
> result in death.

Since the case of Karen Ann Quinlan, this right has been extended to those who are not able to make decisions for themselves; people who have been close to someone who is incompetent or unconscious may use the substituted judgment standard and ask for the kind of care that they know the patient would have wanted. Since the enactment of the PSDA, medical personnel have given information about advance directives to patients and their families as a matter of course.

But problems exist, and one is that when we are hospitalized, the stress of illness makes decision-making difficult. Then, the PSDA is more honored in the breach than the observance because in sickness and even in health, many of us are not aware of our longstanding rights and of the act's legal force. Naive and uninformed, we fail to insist on what we want for ourselves and leave all decision-making to the authorities trained in medical and nursing schools.

Another difficulty, surely thornier than our own reluctance to face mortality, is the reluctance of doctors to do so. The 1995 SUPPORT study notes that, when hospitalized, people who have advance directives are given precisely the same treatment as those who don't. These problems are, however, amenable to resolution. First, why wait until hospitalization creates need for an advance directive? Information may be dealt out ahead of time by the trinity of home, school, and place of worship, and we may certainly write out our wishes well ahead of time. We—and the word "we" includes doctors and other medical personnel—also need to overcome our reluctance to talk about end-of-life issues while we are still full of get-up-and-go. If some people, and not just the disabled, feel unprotected, fearful that someone else will judge their lives, it may well be because they themselves have not specified precisely what they want in a legal document, like a PDA, that's put on file with both doctors and family. We also need to be vocal, speaking loudly and often about our wishes to family members, friends, and the medical establishment. We can protect ourselves if we know enough to do so.

It is with great joy that I hear Dr. Sachedina's criteria for judging the quality of anyone's life. Objective guidelines do exist, and they are three in number. The first is based on connectedness: How well is a person connected with the rest of the human world, with family, friends, neighbors, and community? He says, "You can live as a poor person if you are connected with people. You can live in a very small, dingy place with meager provisions, but it's okay as long as you have people around you. You are connected, and people are there to share with you. The moment you become alone, you have lost an important quality of being a human being because a human being is, by definition, a connected being. Man is a social animal. The modern society seems to be talking about autonomy in the sense of a lonely individual who has no connections, apparently, but they are forgetting that he or she has a connection. It's not an independent individual whose freedom must be protected." We are all, then, part of a larger community that exists beyond our own finite skins. The quality of our lives may be properly measured by the strength of our connectedness to other people. "*You* help people," he says in his gentle voice. "You have connections who will come to *your* help even if you are mentally incapacitated. They will take charge. In your own interest, they will work."

The second criterion is, as Dr. Sachedina puts it, "the functioning of the mental faculty, your ability to make your own decisions rather than being in a state where decisions are made by someone else." So, if you cannot make your own decisions, your quality of life is definitely compromised. You live or die by the strength of your connections to the larger world, which do remain, though reason vanishes.

The third element is material well-being—how much you can afford. "You see," he says, "until the modern medicine started this phenomenal advancement in prolonging life, in prolonging the chances of invasive treatment, traditional societies handed their medicine into the hands of God. You do what you can, then give it into the hands of God. The death took its own natural course, and the person died." He shakes his head and speaks of the Islamic principle of "no harm, no harassment" by which a patient has the right to reject invasive treatment, nor can a doctor insist that it be accepted. "The quality is also measured in affordability. We are introducing all kinds of treatments, nothing is working, the time has come to give up and say, 'Let the nature take its own course, and leave my family alone.' Death is a blessing from God, according to Islam." Connectedness plays a part here, too: to what extent will treatment, especially futile treatment, impoverish a family? As one Muslim publication puts it, we must do our best "in maintaining life *within the limits of knowledge and financial resources.* If an *affordable* medical treatment is available, it must be administered to the patient provided it does not expose the patient to unusual pains and suffering." (The italics are mine.) So affordability—the state of the exchequer—does play a role in determining quality of life, not just for a patient but also for his or her connections.

It strikes me that considerations of affordability are common in making many kinds of financial decisions—a car, a house, a vacation, a dress for the prom. Costs are often a factor in determining the treatment to be given to a pet animal. Only with decision-making in regard to human beings is affordability often tossed out of the equation. But it is not crass—rather it is practical—to take costs into account, for expensive treatments and debt affect a family as well as an individual. Last Acts' study, *Means to a Better End: A Report on Dying in America Today,* issued just before Thanksgiving, 2002, has this to say: "Compared to traditional care for the terminally ill, hospice care and the use of advance directives such as living wills and medical powers of attorney could save up to 10 percent of the cost of care in a patient's last year of life, 10 to 17 percent in the last six months, and 25 to 40 percent in the final month. Traditional care seriously affects family income and savings."

But there's a caution here: Sometimes, the choices of treatment for human beings—what is to be applied and what withheld— depend more on the availability of insurance moneys than on a family's desires. (Many health-maintenance organizations are such notorious penny-pinchers that treatable illness is frequently under- treated or not treated at all.) And the costs of home-care can be a slick, quick road to impoverishment for they are not covered by Medicare and only occasionally by other health insurance, except for the kind of long-term-care policy that contains a home-care provision. At present, families are often caught in a ruinous bind. Marilyn Webb states the problem cogently:

> Although families bear the impact of extended
> treatment most heavily, they have had to fight to
> influence treatment decisions. And instead of estab-
> lishing support systems for beleaguered families,
> our society has brought forth phalanxes of lawyers,
> ethicists, physicians, and social commentators
> who threaten to put limits on the kinds of medical
> choices families can and cannot make, and to moni-
> tor them if they suspect abuse of service or even
> of the patients themselves.

Connectedness, mental alertness, and costs that are not just tol- erable but may result in your improvement—these are dependable rules for judging the quality of life, be it yours or that of some- one else. And be prepared to do battle.

JUST AS the quality of life is now a matter of great concern, so is the quality of death. After a century of dramatically increasing life spans because of the exponential growth of medicine and technology, we have begun to realize that more than two-thirds of us are doomed to die alone in a hospital or other institution rather than at home with connections present—family and sometimes counselors and clergy. A theme common to the stories that friends and strangers have told me about caring for their parents is that the parents did not die alone, for someone who loved them was with them to the end. We who are living and we who are dying are also aided by hospice to achieve such an outcome. Recently, the search for a connectedness in death and dying has taken on a new aspect with entrepreneurs—compassionate, to be sure, but entrepreneurs nonetheless—who have developed a new service industry: assisting the dying and their families with end-of-life issues. Such services include everything imaginable: spiritual guidance and prayer; counseling; meditation techniques for being calm when faced with death; funeral planning; the provision of a cardboard box for a body destined for the crematory or dry ice to preserve a body through visitation and the wake to interment; and a host of other options. Most at this point are shoestring operations, with many of them found—where else?—in California, but financier George Soros has founded and supported the Project on Death in America, which conducts research on how best to handle the "physical, emotional, existential, and spiritual" dimensions of dying. Its mission statement is worth repeating:

> The mission of the Project on Death in America is
> to understand and transform the culture and experi-
> ence of dying and bereavement through initiatives
> in research, scholarship, the humanities, and the

arts, and to foster innovations in the provision of
care, public education, professional education, and
public policy.

Innovations in public policy—here's a strong effort to restore
decision-making to its proper sphere, to the family and doctors
familiar with the patient. The Project publishes a newsletter,
which is available over the Internet. Then, in 2000, Bill Moyers
aired his notable documentary on the quality of death—"On Our
Own Terms," which examines the ways in which a diverse group
of terminally ill people came to grips with their mortality. Watching it, sometimes moved to tears, I noted, however, that only one
of them was not able to make his own decisions—a man in a coma,
whose wife acted as his proxy. The irrational or comatose are
often invisible to the rest of us. Nonetheless, the documentary is
worth watching over and over again, for, among other virtues, it
presents a hospice in action and covers the deliberations of an
Oregon woman, bald from chemotherapy intended to quell cancer, who had opted for assisted suicide but died before she could
activate her request.

    The quality of death concerns James LaGrua, my mother's
physician. I meet with him in his office on a chilly November
afternoon. The office, however, is warm, not only in temperature
but in décor. A huge round Coca-Cola sign, white letters on red,
dominates one wall, while another beside his desk holds a big bul-
letin board featuring pictures of his family. His smile is as broad
and welcoming as ever. When he speaks about any subject that
deeply engages him, his voice rises with a boyish intensity. We
first discuss the meaning of the term "quality of life." He says, "It's
whatever the patient says it is. As physicians, we have our own
prejudices and will often convey it to our patients." He tells an

illustrative story. One of his patients now housed in a nursing home, a man who never knew many comforts in life, suffers from ALS, Lou Gehrig's disease. The progress of the disease is such that near the end, paralysis robs a person of the ability to breathe on his own and swallow his saliva; the only thing that he can still achieve is moving his eyeballs. But before his patient reached that point—when he was still able to communicate slightly—Dr. LaGrua asked him how long he wanted to be kept alive, expecting that he'd say that when all he could do was roll his eyes, that would be it—let him go. But his answer was, "Keep me alive as long as you possibly can." One day when Dr. LaGrua was making rounds at the nursing home, he saw his patient watching the "Scooby-Doo" show on television. "I made the observation that for some people, sitting in a bed and having nurses attend to you and watching 'Scooby-Doo' makes for a good quality of life by their definition. But we ask the patient at which point do you or do you not want us to continue artificial or aggressive life support. Most people say differently than this gentleman. But quality of life is whatever they define it as. We'd be too bold if we tried to define it for them."

He shakes his head and his voice rises in pitch when he talks about the problems that he as a physician encounters at nursing homes. As with my friend Nancy's mother, such institutions are reluctant, sometimes quite unwilling, to consider palliative care because to let someone die can be read as dire neglect of a patient's well-being. He tells a tale that amply documents his point. A nursing-home administrator asked him to contact the family of a patient who was frail and severely demented. Even though she was being given medication to increase her appetite, her weight had gone down below a hundred pounds because she ate so little. The administrator also wanted him to document in the chart that he had suggested a feeding tube to the family because of the extreme weight loss. But what he documented was this: "She's deteriorating, she has advanced Alzheimer's, and I don't believe a feeding tube is appropriate or ethical." He adds, "Nursing homes are not allowed to let people go peacefully. It's not looked on favorably. The press talks of starvation, but the people who write these stories haven't quite grasped that these people are withering away, losing the will to eat. Every nursing home is afraid of being charged with neglect, and they err on the side that if something happens, you have to jump on it. We can't say we're not going to treat the next infection. Public policy does not really ensure us any safety if we allow a person to go because we and the family think it's time to go."

The other problem that nursing homes face is that they are breeding grounds for resistant organisms through the massive prescribing of antibiotics. "It's not from prescribing too much penicillin for strep throat; it's from prescribing gorilla antibiotics to people whom we know we won't cure. That's what causes the resistance. And we do it because it's demanded. The patients or their families are saying, 'Do it.'" Unfortunately, disease-causing agents have strong survival instincts; those that manage to live through the battles with antibiotics reproduce organisms as vital and determined as themselves.

Dr. LaGrua sees the pros and cons of withdrawing life support as Lynn Coyner does. "People are on life support rarely because of their own wishes. It's because of family members who have unresolved psychological issues. And you can see it. There's anger, there's loss, there's guilt. People who have great relationships with their mothers and fathers don't keep them alive on life support or with heroic measures. And the ones who do—you can see there are secrets there." Great relationships are also important, and not just among parents and children but also between family and physician. It's another term for connectedness, Dr. Sachedina's number-one criterion for determining the quality of life.

"I want to give you a thought," he says. "There's something to be said for quality of death. Few people ever plan for the quality of their death. Oh, every now and then, but it's rare. Unfortunately, most people die not in good quality-of-death situations." The kind of death that he thinks is blessed happens when someone is so ill that death will occur after a short time, but consciousness has been retained. Then, Dr. LaGrua rallies the family. "They all come in," he says, "and they get that blessing of being able to spend time with their loved ones, still aware. They know they are dying, the family is there, and everybody shares in the death experience. They don't fight it. They share."

On the other hand, coding can make for the kind of quality of death that no one ever wishes for. Code Blue stipulates that when someone's heart is in arrest and emergency technicians are called in, they must make every attempt at resuscitation. If someone is coded, then it entails CPR, mechanical ventilation, and shocking. Dr. LaGrua's experience is that people in good health, or even in bad health but with sturdy hearts, will ask to be jump-started. But for someone who is elderly, with advanced heart disease, it is not remotely likely to be successful. "It will result in a painful death. We try to talk them out of it." The active word here is *try*. The wishes of patient and family must be honored, even if the doctor disagrees.

His thoughts on getting ready for death are worth recounting. "It's not usually a problem," he says. "Illness wears you down and gives you a sense of the reality. When we try to prepare patients for death and talk about planning for it, they're usually ready because they've been worn down for months or years. By the time we approach it, when we say we need to get ready for the end, they're usually a bit relieved." On the other hand, preparing for death and even contemplating mortality is almost impossible for people still in good health. "It's not real till you feel your strength sapping away, till you feel the ravages of illness. Then it becomes real, and most people who reach that point accept it."

I find his thoughts solacing. He has deeply pondered the issues we talk about, and I wish that all patients could find someone like him, both eager to heal and quick to comfort.

MARCH: Sarah is eighty-six. For someone in her condition, for anyone whose mind, once smoothly oiled, has seized up, it is possible to assess quality of life. She remains connected, although she is not fully aware of the people in orbit around her, and she can neither direct them nor ask for their help. The main criterion in her case is mental impairment, which robs her of purpose, and without purpose, without a shred of ability to form it, her life has been stripped of meaning. She has no access to selfhood, for it has long since departed. No doubt about it, she is well cared for, but she has no role to play, except that, as Rosa puts it, of a rag doll. Nor does she know whether she's in her own home or in Timbuktu. I get a close view of her descent into total ignorance, for I am weeks late in making my annual spring migration south to North Carolina. The reason: I am undergoing radiation treatments after a lumpectomy removed cancerous tissue from my left breast. Her ignorance leads me to think that the time has truly come to move her to a nursing home.

Money (the third of Dr. Sachedina's criteria, as I'll learn much later) plays a part in my pondering, as it should whenever a family faces expenses that erode resources like huge waves relentlessly gnawing away at a shoreline. My sisters, brothers, and I have long believed that, like our father and grandmother, she should die at home. But keeping her at home with round-the-clock care has turned out to be an extremely expensive proposition. And if a worthy facility can be found, one that offers cleanliness, respect, kindness, and good cheer, then she would be cared for as well as she is at home and at far less cost so that her much diminished assets would be made to last longer. We have been fortunate, though, compared with other families faced with overwhelming, too often ruinous end-of-life costs, for Sarah was left well provided for when her husband, Joe, died.

Though I do not speak with my siblings about moving Sarah to a nursing home, I do discuss these thoughts with Dr. LaGrua. In a gentle but definite voice, he says, "She has no quality of life. For a woman who has done a lot in her life, has been successful and active, she has nothing left." Suddenly, I feel bolstered: This is the first time that someone who can view the situation with objectivity has used the term "quality of life" to me and noted its absence in Sarah's constricted circumstances. We talk about her tears and sadness, her helplessness, her irrationality, and the fear that it engenders because she understands little or nothing of what we tell her. Nor does she have the power to adapt; that left her years ago. She is like a chipped and empty shell cast up on a beach. Dr. LaGrua gives the nursing-home idea his full support.

My agenda is set: visits to local nursing homes in the morning, radiation treatments in the afternoon. Some facilities have reputations for odors, sloppy care, and medicating aggressive patients into drug-bloated somnolence. They do not make my list of places to see. To avoid preemptive arguments, I scout some of the area's other nursing homes without consulting my sisters and brothers. This time around, they will simply be informed of a fait accompli.

Visiting the facilities takes me over the entire county, the second largest in Virginia and close to 1,000 square miles. Those with stellar reputations have long waiting lists. Waiting, however, would simply maintain the status quo. I fall back on Blue Sky Manor, which has openings and is familiar to us, for it was the nursing home in which Sarah stayed, biding her time between hospitalization after the second stroke and entry into the rehabilitation center's program. On March 24, I fill out the admissions forms. On March 27, I send a check to bind the contract. On March 28, I finally tell my siblings and the three caregivers that Sarah will go to Blue Sky Manor on April 9. My brothers and sisters are not enthusiastic but give assent. Two of the caregivers sigh heavily and accept this turn of events. They'll have no trouble finding jobs elsewhere. But Rosa fights.

She has vested time, energy, and love into her work. She has cared for Sarah tenderly for five-and-a-half years. Her patient is clean and well-fed. And she's right proud of being the head caregiver, the woman who made it possible for Sarah to stay at home. It is not the disappearance of a job that distresses her but rather the possibility that Blue Sky Manor will not afford Sarah the kind of care, the special all-attentive care, to which she is accustomed, and that it will not seek to keep her fears from rising. Rosa conducts an investigation and, behold, discovers that Blue Sky Manor has committed many violations of the state codes governing nursing homes, from serious understaffing to omission of necessary sterilization procedures. Nor have all the violations been corrected. She broadcasts her findings to anyone who will listen, from family to the handful of visitors who still make an effort to bring fresh flowers or homemade goodies. I cannot deny that Rosa has a point: Blue Sky Manor, despite giving Sarah a satisfactory way station while she was caught in the limbo between hospital and rehab, is not a truly suitable place for her now. She needs reliable long-term care. What to do? The time for transition has come, but I've spun my wheels and nothing has been accomplished. I consult my triumvirate of attorney, accountant, and banker: Do they know of local facilities that I might look into? Yes, St. Luke's, eight miles down the pike, which bills itself not as a nursing home but rather as a "long-term care facility, nursing home alternative." Why didn't *I* think of that? The family certainly knows of St. Luke's, for an aunt, the widow of my mother's brother, has been living there for at least the last three years. I call my aunt's younger sister, who gives it accolades for care and cleanliness. It is privately owned, not part of a chain, and, run by its proprietors, it houses thirty-six patients at most. When I visit, I note that the place is immaculate and bright, with pastel walls and flowered chintz bedspreads and curtains. The attitude on the part of the staff is one of happy industry; the tidy patients are engaged in activities from conversation to singing to catnapping. A long day room with views of the Blue Ridge provides comfortable recliners from which the halt and infirm can cozily watch television. I learn, too, that St. Luke's will honor both Sarah's living will and DNR, and she would not be taken to the hospital except for something like a cut that could be mended or a broken osteoporotic bone that could be set to make her more comfortable. Palliative care—that's the commandment. And, yes, St. Luke's has an opening. With proper paperwork, Sarah can move in on April 9.

Radiation treatments at an end, I make a quick trip to my home in North Carolina but return for the grand move on April 9. The caregivers have been busy indeed, labeling everything from nightgowns and underclothes to slippers and the comfortably loose-fitting jumpers that Sarah usually wears. All of these things have been carefully packed in cardboard cartons. Except for Rosa, the caregivers, wearing an air of sad resignation, make doubly sure to let the family know that they have felt privileged to attend to Sarah's every need. Rosa will stay on for three more weeks, visiting St. Luke's daily and helping Sarah cope with any adjustment problems that may show up. Meanwhile, I confer with a real estate agent, for Sarah's townhouse will go on the market as soon as it has been vacated.

A few days before the move, Sarah goes to the radiology department at the hospital for an x-ray of her lungs. Then, on the morning of the move, Dr. LaGrua gives her a physical exam, fills out the nursing home's standard form, and makes a list of her medications—a very short list that includes only vitamins and Dilantin. In the afternoon, when she's finished her postprandial nap, Sarah is dressed and wheeled outside to Rosa's van, which has already been packed with the cardboard cartons of clothing. Wheelchair folded and stashed in the back, off they go. They lead a procession: Joe, Bob's wife, and I follow, each in our separate cars. Once at St. Luke's, Sarah is wheeled into her room—its primary color is sunshine yellow—and we unpack her things, while the proprietors and aides come flocking around. Sarah, the center of attention, is beaming. It is impossible to know what notions or visions, if any, go through her head. But my impression is that she somehow feels that she's been taken to a grand party. For someone as sociable as she was in her former life, coming to St. Luke's seems a treat of the highest order.

When I return to North Carolina, I feel assured that she will be well cared for, especially with no-nonsense Rosa on board, nor will family abandon her. Joe visits daily, as he always has, and others come with only slightly less frequency. My distant sisters stay in touch by telephone. Sarah may not understand what is being said to her, but she knows by heart the sound of a loving human voice. When Rosa leaves at the end of three weeks, she tells us that she thinks that Sarah has noticed a change in her surroundings, but she's not sure. Sarah's sadness has diminished; she seems content. Not much later, however, an aide calls me: My mother has taken a tumble from the bed to the floor; it would be preferable not to leave her alone but to take her to the hospital to see if there are serious injuries. I assent because such a trip falls into the category of checking for problems that can be remedied. A week later when I come north to clean out her townhouse, furniture to kitchenware to linens to doodads, and close on its sale, I go to see her. Wearing her Sunday-go-to-meeting best, she sits in a recliner in the dayroom. Her right eye is decked with a gorgeous purple-black shiner. But she is smiling. The quality of her life has definitely improved, for sorrow is no longer her constant companion. Nonetheless, she will never again be capable of rational thought and purposeful action. I tell her of my travels and of giving some of her most treasured furniture—a Victorian chest of drawers, a card table topped with glass-covered needle-point, a framed piece of Chinese embroidery—to my sisters and sisters-in-law. In a gentle voice, she says, "Good, good." Those are the last words I shall ever hear her say.

The promise that I made nine years ago to help her die is at last being fulfilled. There is a decided difference between being kept alive and being allowed to die. My mother has left her home in which the continuation of her life was paramount. But now she is in a place that will let her dying take its natural course. She will go gently into that good night.

Freedom

At the last, tenderly,
From the walls of the powerful fortress'd house,
From the clasp of the knitted locks, from the keep
    of the well-closed doors,
Let me be wafted.

          —Walt Whitman, "The Last Invocation"

I AM AT my home in North Carolina on July 5, 1998 when a nursing home staff member telephones: Sarah has closed her eyes and will not open her mouth. The moment has finally come. Her five-and-a-half-year travail is nearly at an end. Three weeks after her eighty-seventh birthday, she is close to making the tremendous transition from the world of the living to the realm of the dead. The nursing staff is doing exactly as I'd asked, letting her go in peace rather than trying to rouse her or take her to the hospital. And when she does die, at 1:35 P.M. the next day, I am on the road driving north. The car radio, tuned to NPR, reports the death on this very same day of the silver-screen cowboy Roy Rogers. As the miles roll by, I find that my mother's death brings me relief rather than sadness. Nor is this feeling odd, for most of my mourning was accomplished while she lived. I find myself rejoicing that the nursing home proprietors and staff understood that the goal was to keep Sarah comfortable rather than strive for a cure that would, though only for a little while, keep mortality at bay. They have given her the tenderest care, a large part of which was simply not to interfere as her life waned. Joe is with her when she breathes her last. He tells me later that he, too, felt relief, for no one—not anyone, ever—should be subjected to such protracted dying.

Long ago, Sarah requested cremation, making sure that all her children knew of her wishes, and the nursing home was so informed. By the time I reach Staunton, her body has been transported to the funeral home that handled the arrangements for my father's cremation and my grandmother's burial. Stopping there before I go to my house, I learn something I had not known. I do know that my legally granted powers to represent her ended the instant that she died. But it is a startlement to be told by the funeral home's proprietor that my word alone is not enough to allow them to proceed with her cremation. All five of us must agree that cremation is what *we* wish, and each of us must present a written statement to that effect. Why? It seems that a spouse may speak for a spouse, and a parent for a child, even a grown child, as I did for my daughter Hannah, but when a widowed parent dies without ever authorizing cremation, all the children must concur in writing that cremation is desired. Nor is such authorization merely a crochet of this particular undertaking parlor. The Federal Trade Commission, the Board of Funeral Homes, and other official bodies have made it a rule. The objective is to protect both the customer and the funeral home lest disagreement lead to a lawsuit. The three of us who live in town give our consent the same afternoon. The two who live far afield send their yeses by fax. Joe picks up the ashes several days later, and we make arrangements for a memorial service at the church where Sarah long served as an elder.

The chosen day, July 18, dawns fair. And at the chosen hour, 11:00 A.M., the church is packed, standing room only, for a service that lasts almost an hour. Afterward, the ladies of the church provide a fine cold spread—meat, cheeses, bread, homemade biscuits, grapes and melon balls, cookies and brownies, and gallons of iced tea. Then, at 2:30, Sarah's family takes her on her last earthly journey. Three generations of us assemble at the foot of her favorite hill, the one that the Valley's first Scotch-Irish settlers named Betsey Bell after a legendary Scottish maiden. The story has it that, when the plague struck near Perth, Scotland, in 1645, Betsey and her best friend, Mary Gray, were sent into a bower specially built as a refuge by their fathers, the lairds, respectively, of Kinvaid and Lednoch. But a suitor, said to have been smitten by both girls, followed them, and the plague traveled with him. So much for paternal caution: The girls died.

Here in the Valley, the wooded, rounded hill known as Betsey Bell stands intimately next to a slightly smaller twin named for Mary Gray. Betsey belongs to the town now and is minimally maintained as a public park. Curving up through dense woods on one side, then descending on the other, the road is steep and pitted with axel-punishing ruts. At the top, however, the town has erected a twenty-by-twenty-foot platform with benches and a railing. On the side facing east, the trees on the hillside have been cut away to provide a view of the Blue Ridge Mountains. The view that Sarah treasured was that of Betsey Bell, and she made sure that she could see its green and gentle rise from any house in which she lived.

Joe puts her ashes, packaged in a clear plastic wrapper enclosed in a small, rectangular brown box, into his backpack. Some of us—all of the children, running and skipping, and the younger adults, some huffing and puffing—accompany him on the mile-long trek up the hill. The rest of us are variously chauffeured to the top in four-wheel-drive SUVs. That includes me, for the osteoarthritic knee is not up to hill-climbing, or, for that matter, to flatland walking.

Though we've kept it mostly to family—the crowd at the memorial service was not invited—the assemblage shows the ecumenicalism of Sarah's life. She knew no boundaries; she regularly crossed all lines. Rosa and the other black caregiver are here on Betsey Bell, as are Jerry and his wife, Donna, both originally from Taiwan, along with their two black-haired, sloe-eyed, American-born youngsters. More than a decade ago, under the auspices of a church-sponsored international students' program, Jerry, who was working towards a degree in urban planning at an American university and would have found it difficult to make the trip home during vacation, came to stay with her over Christmas; he returned the following summer to serve an internship with the town's government. After that he kept in close touch, and when his daughter was born, she was named Sarah. As for the rest of us, all five of her children are present, along with four of the eleven grandchildren and three of the nine great-grands. And we're here with a fine assortment of spouses, uncles, aunts, and cousins, who have traveled from Maine, New Hampshire, Massachusetts, upper New York state, and Florida for this occasion.

The shade of the trees is sweet on this July afternoon, as is the softly stirring breeze. We have also been granted music. Somewhere on the hillside, a wood thrush repeats and repeats the triplets of its heart-haunting song. The moment has come. I read a few lines from one of Sarah's poems:

The golden sunset
Not the glare of sun
Blue haze on mountain
Not toilsome upward trail

She has finished her journey and reached the sunset.

Facing the Blue Ridge, Joe stands against the platform's railing. He opens the brown box, then the plastic bag containing our mother's ashes, and shakes them gently onto the hillside. I note that no one's crying. Instead, everyone smiles. We are there to celebrate Sarah's life, not to mourn her death. Our mourning was done long ago, when she ceased to live though she was still alive. Now she has not died, she's been set free. With celebration uppermost in mind, Joe's younger son, Jim, has brought along a bottle of single-malt Scotch whisky and a Mason jar to drink it from. He fills the jar, which makes the rounds. When all who wish to sip have done so—and almost everybody does so wish, Joe offers Sarah a libation, pouring the last drops on her ashes. And we descend. The wood thrush is still singing.

That evening, my husband, the Chief, and I hold a wake at our house. Or I suppose it's a wake, but it looks more like a big spaghetti supper with much conversation in the kitchen, in the living room, and on the front porch. The night is filled with reminiscence, family anecdotes, tales of things past, hopes of things to be. We are suffused, too, with a sense that we've done the right thing. The celebration continues unabated. I don't know when it ends, for I go to bed when my eyelids start to register at half-mast. Sleep is completely sound.

Afterwards, whenever I look at Betsey Bell or see a rainbow, I think, There she is. That green hill, that radiant arc are our touchpoints, the place to which we may go physically or in our minds to remember her. And I smile.

In the End, Which Is Also a Beginning

Ho bios brakhys, e de tekhne makre, ho de kairos oxys,
e de peira sphalere, e de krisis khalepe.
Art lasts, but life doesn't; opportunity's here and
gone, with experimentation likely to trip you
up, and decision-making damned hard.

—Hippocrates, *Aphorisms*

MY MOTHER'S five-and-a-half-year ordeal has stimulated talk and action as well as thought. Though her caregivers were skilled professionals, the rest of us who cared for her proceeded by guess and by golly, and our tutelary spirit was Epimetheus, the god of hindsight.

What could we have done that was different from what we did? What can anyone do who deals with damaged, demented brains, be it from strokes, Alzheimer's disease, or senility stealthily advancing from other causes? Not much, except for one thing—and it is everything: seek to comfort, not to cure. *Comfort*—the word comes from Latin and means "strengthen greatly," and the strength is spiritual, bringing peace. It's senseless to say that we should have let her die before she did—die of the second stroke, die of pneumonia, die of refusing to eat or drink, for the point is now moot. The living often find letting go to be an act as difficult as balancing an egg or carrying water in a sieve. But the lessons that we learned are worth recounting briefly. And they came on two levels. One addresses the best way to care for someone loved and death-bound whose mind is gone, though spirit and flesh are still present. The other has to do with those of us who are still feisty.

For my mother, as with others whose minds have slipped away, I know that two things are paramount in bestowing tender care: voice and touch. A calm, happy voice makes a gift of its emotional content to the hearer, even though there may be no comprehension of what the words mean. When one of the caregivers picked up on reading to Sarah after I'd left off, almost miraculously, the stream of soft words dried her tears, at least for that half-hour, and gave her repose. And she was just as soothed if someone patted her hand, stroked her arm, or, best of all, rubbed lotion on her feet. I do not know for certain how touch and voice work to produce a peacefulness but think that it has to do with keeping an old, frail person connected with the rest of humankind. Keeping a regular routine also helps. My mother in the dark, haunted woods of her dementia was like a pet animal, trained to expect both basic necessities—food, bathing, sleep—and amenities, like visits, television-watching, and wheelchair rides, at a set time every day. Of course, there were occasional breaks in routine—pleasant outings, along with trips to the doctor or dentist—but they did not upset her if familiar faces and voices accompanied her. On the practical side, I've also learned that a nursing home is not at all a last resort but rather a workable option, especially if constant care or vigilance is needed. Nor is placement in such a facility something that should bring guilt. Guilt often comes, as Lynn Coyner and James LaGrua say, when the living have unfinished business with the dying. That there may be unfinished business constitutes a brief for upfront honesty in dealing with other people, and it serves as a warning that we not dillydally, putting off resolving problems, until it's too late to finish anything. And economic factors may also be legitimately taken into consideration. Which is worse—a family's ruination or the provision of palliative care in a home, a nursing facility, or a hospital?

Palliative care, it must be noted, is something fairly new; the first modern textbook on the subject did not appear until 1993. According to the 2002 report *Means to a Better End*, the principles of palliative care are fivefold: It "respects the goals, likes, and choices of the dying person; looks after the medical, emotional, social and spiritual needs of the dying person; supports the needs of family members; helps gain access to needed health-care providers and appropriate care settings; and builds ways to provide excellent care at the end of life." A commonsensical prescription and one that is surely easiest on the pocketbook, but the 2002 figures show that in the last months of life, the high-tech road to death commands the greatest percentage of the money that is spent on every aspect of health care. And to what end? To buy another month? The problem boils down to one of decision-making: Who calls the shots? A poll conducted on the Internet by the *Wall Street Journal* in 2001 asked readers, "Who should decide when to discontinue treatment because of costs?" Hospital administrators received a trifling three percent of the vote; doctors, 24 percent; insurance companies, seven percent; and patients or their families, a whopping 65 percent.

The relief of pain is paramount in palliative care, and most pain is amenable to treatment. It's not always possible, however, for a physician to administer the necessary drugs. The reason lies with state policies and laws in regard to controlled substances. With the laudable intent of preventing overprescription and addiction,

186 The Quality of Life

states have variously and unwittingly set in place obstacles to adequate pain control for seriously ill and dying people. Last Acts' 2002 report puts it this way: "Some of these state policies are useful and effective; some create formidable barriers to good pain management. For example, certain laws would sanction a doctor based on the number of doses in a prescription or the prescription's duration, both of which standards have no clinical basis and do not take into account the very high doses some patients may need." Here is a call as unsettling as a siren for us, the patients and families, to take political action.

We have to be tough, for it may well be necessary to fight for the comfort of someone we love who is dying. Time and again, in talking about end-of-life issues with people, like my friends Nancy, Margaret, and Marguerite, I hear them wax exceeding wroth about the difficulties that they've had in dealing with health-care professionals. They've had to battle the establishment in order to stave off the high-tech approach, when all that was wanted was comfort for their mothers and the honoring of maternal wishes. Another friend, recent victim of a broken ankle, writes of her not-to-be-dismissed notion that it's important "to learn to operate within the medical system as it now is. For a person getting older, this may rate as an essential survival skill, along with operating an ATM machine." To this, I add that it's wise to go for a second opinion, especially in regard to the elderly and frail.

Many of us, however, are laggards. We must first come to grips with the fact that a futile moment always comes, a time at which artifice should be abandoned and nature allowed to take over. The questions are: Is there a chance for the patient's healing? If not, what is necessary for the patient's comfort? Above all, we need to talk about death and dying well before those moments come. As Josephine Jacobsen has written in her poem "The Companions," fraternization "with the dark prince is possible and wise," for life and death cannot be separated.

My mother's long years of decline have affected me and my immediate family in ways that I could not possibly have predicted before she lost her health. Until that time, terminal illness and death did not figure in my calculations except as matters of theory, not reality. Then, in the 1990s, death came quietly closer and closer still. 1992: My mother suffered her first stroke; struck by intimations of her mortality, I wept as the ambulance took us over the Blue Ridge Mountains to the hospital in Charlottesville. 1994: the first to die was our beloved Doberman, Sally, a faithful partner who figured often in my stories. 1995: My daughter Hannah lost her battle with cancer. 1998: My mother finally achieved her freedom. 2002: my husband, the Chief, made his *transitus* after a long bout with cirrhosis, a disease that wasted his flesh and robbed him of energy, though it left his mind largely intact. But in the course of his dying, I was comforted because we had discussed end-of-life issues throughout the years of my mother's downhill slide. Because her situation had prompted us to talk day in and day out, each of us knew what the other wished for. And because I knew, I could keep faith with his stated requests so that it was easier to let him go, to say goodbye.

What had he requested? To begin with, he made a living will stipulating that he wanted a natural death, not artificial prolongation of a waning life by tubes and respirators. His deepest desire was to stay at home to the end with hospice care. When it became evident a month before his death that he could no longer climb stairs and was also having difficulty walking, we turned the living room into his special place. We moved the sofa into the large front hall and brought in a walker, a portable commode, an over-the-bed table on wheels, and a hospital bed with three motors that could raise and lower the whole mattress, as well as either of its ends. There he stayed for the last month of his life, surrounded not just by these new things but also his television set and his huge collection of John Wayne movies—148 of the 150-plus that the quintessential cowboy-warrior made. And the Chief could move from the bed to his plush recliner, equipped with heat and vibration. When it became hard for me to help him move from bed to chair and back—he was a heavy man—we called in hospice. Women and more women—he'd always liked women, and here they were, a whole bevy of them, talking with him, bathing him, and generally making a big cheerful fuss. Day and night, he wandered in and out of sleep, and his conversation dwindled to the point of asking only, "What's for supper?" But several days before he died, he got a devilish look in his eye when the aide washed his chest. "What the hell!" he said, smiling and enjoying every second of this gentle attention. I knew, too, that he wanted cremation, with his ashes scattered in the wide and salty river Neuse that flows only seventy-five feet from our front door in North Carolina, the river that he'd fished and boated and swum in, that he listened to after dark in his front-yard swing as the wavelets lapped against the seawall. And that's what was done. Family, neighbors, and friends gathered on a fair Sunday in May. Some made memorial remarks. As I scattered the ashes, Jeffery Beam, whose poem serves as the epigraph for the second chapter in this book, sang "Parting Friends," an old shape-note song from the 1840s. It tells of someone leaving (in a Conestoga wagon?) and not likely to be seen again, except in Canaan Land, a place of God-promised rest. That done, several guests sailed red roses into the river, while others poured libations of Miller High Life, the Chief's favorite beer. We adjourned then for a potluck feast. I had a strong feeling that his spirit was indeed stirring happily among us because he had given me most specific guidance on what he wished, and his wishes had been honored. Like my mother's memorial, the occasion was a celebration of his life, not a lamentation and a grieving for his death. My touch-point is the river: I see or think of it and he is present in my memory.

And as he told me what he wished, so I have told my children, not just in words but also in writing. They know to put my ashes in the Bullpasture River, which flows in the western part of Virginia where the terrain looks as if a divine fist has closed around the land and crumpled it into mountains. They know, too, what they should do before that final moment. I've long had a will and have also made both a business power of attorney and a DPA. I've made arrangements and paid for my cremation; my children will not have to get together and agree to it after I die because I've already signed the authorization form, which is on file at the funeral home. (A cautionary note is needed here: check the pertinent laws of your state, for they show wide variation. The disposal of remains can be contentious, and living family members may be the ones who decide the issue, no matter how often and forcefully you've expressed your wishes. In Louisiana, for one, your wishes will be honored after your death if they have been written out and notarized, while in Ohio, although you may formally authorize cremation, a surviving spouse may override your intent, and in West Virginia, your wishes will prevail only if you've made payment for your funeral before your death.) I've also taken out a long-term care insurance policy. When I become a different person, as my mother did, I may kick and scream at the very notion of a nursing home, but now I am in full possession of my mind and senses and have put my wishes in writing. My children have been instructed, too, to fight for palliative care on my behalf if I cannot do so myself. Perhaps in the near future, comfort care will be more widely practiced by medical professionals, who now come down far more often on the side of cure. Inevitably, the time will come that I represent the past; my children, the present; and my children's children, the future. They owe their time, energy, and money to themselves and to the future.

In Sarah's long, slow dying, she taught me how to live. And she taught me something else as well: Just as all life can be considered sacred, so, too, is death. It holds a sanctity no less than that of life.

Resources

Administration on Aging, U.S. Department of Health and Human
    Services, 200 Independence Avenue SW, Room 309, Washing-
    ton, DC; telephone (212) 401-4541; toll-free Eldercare Locator
    (800) 677-1116. Web site: http://www.aoa.gov. The AOA includes
    the National Aging Information Center and a listing of state and
    area agencies.
Aging Network Services, Topaz House, 4400 East-West Highway,
    Bethesda, MD, 20814; telephone (301) 657-4329. Web site:
    http://agingnets.com. The company offers families of patients
    living at home geriatric care management services, some of which
    may be covered by Medicare or long-term care insurance. It has
    also published a useful book, *Coping with Your Difficult Older
    Parent: A Guide for Stressed-Out Children.*
Aging with Dignity, telephone toll-free at (888) 594-7437. Web site:
    http://www.agingwithdignity.org. The organization offers the
    Five Wishes document that gives you a DPA, a living will, two
    sorts of directives on your medical treatment, and a message to
    your survivors; order toll free at (888) 549-7437.

Alzheimer's Association, 919 North Michigan Avenue, Suite 1100, Chicago, IL 60611-1676; telephone (312) 335-8700 or toll-free at (800) 272-3900. Web site: http://www.alz.org. The association offers an array of services that range from supplying reading materials to locating support-group chapters. The association furnishes information not only on Alzheimer's but other dementias.

American Society on Aging, 833 Market Street, Suite 511, San Francisco, CA 94103-1824; telephone (415) 974-9600 or toll-free at (800) 537-9728. Web site: http://www.asaging.org. The society is a source of information for those who give care to older people.

Euthanasia Research and Guidance Organization (ERGO), 24829 Norris Lane, Junction City, OR 97448-9559; telephone (541) 998-1873. Web site: http://www.finalexit.org. ERGO was founded by Derek Humphry, author of *Final Exit*. The full text of the Oregon Death with Dignity Act may be found at this site, which also features material on death by choice, including Humphry's book in an updated edition. A list of right-to-die organizations worldwide is also provided.

Family Caregiver Alliance, 690 Market Street, Suite 600, San Francisco, CA 94104; telephone (415) 434-3388 or toll-free at (800) 445-8106. Web site: http://www.caregiver.org. The alliance's focus is on long-term care at home. In addition to serving people who live in the San Francisco area directly, it also offers publications that are available to caregivers and professionals anywhere, who work with brain-damaged adults.

Last Acts; telephone: (301) 652-1558. Web site: http://www.lastacts.org/files/misc/meansfull.pdf. The organization has issued a report card for end-of-life services offered in each of the fifty states. Most come in at a dismal C-minus. The organization's goal is to encourage change at all levels, including the medical and the legislative, to bring comfort to the dying. Lay people are urged to participate along with professionals.

Lifeline Systems, Inc., 111 Lawrence Street, Framingham, MA 01702-8156; telephone (800) 451-0525. Web site: http://www.lifelinesy.com. The company sells Lifeline disks, small, waterproof units with a central button that an older or ill person may press to summon help in case of an accident, stroke, or other emergency.

National Council on the Aging, 409 3rd Street SW, Suite 200, Washington, DC; telephone (202) 4791200 or toll-free at (800) 424-9046. Web site: http://ncoa.org. The council, which does not respond to individuals, is nonetheless a fine source of information on home care and adult day care. The council also offers a benefits check-up to determine, based on needs and financial situation, if an older adult qualifies for a host of programs offered by federal, state, and local agencies, including services and tax breaks. Web site: http://www.benefitscheckup.org.

National Hospice and Palliative Care Organization, 1700 Diagonal Road, Suite 300, Alexandria, VA 22314; toll-free at (800) 658-8898. Web site: http://www.nhpco.org. This organization, which stems from a cooperative effort between the Administration on Aging and the National Institute on Aging, provides fact sheets and other publications and locates hospice services.

National Institute on Aging, NIA Information Center, P. O. Box 8057, Gaithersburg, MD 20898-8057; toll-free at (800) 222-2225. Web site: http://www.nia.nih.gov. The NIA offers videos and publications dealing with aging, including *The Resource Directory for Older People*. It also lists federal Web sites of interest to older adults.

National Right to Life Committee, 512 10th Street NW, Washington, DC 20004; telephone (212) 626-8800. Web site: http://www.nrlc.org. The committee is concerned with medical ethics relating to end-of-life issues. It is the source for the detailed Will to Live DPA.

National Stroke Association, 96 Inverness Drive East, Suite I, Englewood, CO 80112-5112; telephone (303) 649-9299 or toll-free at (800) 787-6537. Web site: http://www.stroke.org. The association is a trove of information on topics such as stroke prevention, stroke symptoms and effects, acute treatment, and resources for both caregivers and survivors. It also offers a good selection of books and brochures on stroke, and publishes a magazine for a non-professional readership.

Project on Death in America, Open Society Institute, 400 West 59th Street, New York, NY 10019; telephone (212) 548-0150. Web site: http://www.soros.org. The project, which works with professional researchers and educators, initiates investigations of the experience of dying and grief to promote innovations in care, education, and public policy.

Safe Return, P. O. Box 9307, St. Louis, MO 63117-0307; toll-free at (888) 572-8566. Safe Return, organized by the Alzheimer's Association and the National Center for Missing Persons, provides a bracelet to caregivers that may be used for people with dementia. The bracelet is inscribed with the names of patient and caregiver and Safe Return's toll-free number, (800) 572-1122, so that a confused wanderer may be identified and brought safely home.

The Stroke Network; telephone (410) 569-1272. Web site: http:// strokenetwork.org. The network, a strictly online organization, gives support and information to caregivers and survivors. It also provides links to such topics as aphasia and stroke treatment.

Notes

"'In the Beginning"
  O may I join: Eliot quoted by Enright, page 165.

"Death by Choice"
  So proud she was to die: Dickinson, page 207.
  "The problem was that death": Rollin, page 58.
  "What do people do": Rollin, page 216.
  "Sister, dear sister": West, page 113.
  "All of us know": West, page 114.
  "We were planners": West, page 128.
  "adventure of this sacred journey": Wright, page 212.
  On December 7 . . . "thickest and finest": Wright, pages 213–214.
  "These were pragmatic": Moore, page 81.
  "Mercy killing": Moore, page 87.
  "Mercy Living": Lagnado, all quotations from *The Wall Street Journal*, page 20.
  "You had the audacity": ABCNews.com.
  A study published in 2002: Britten.
  'Assisting': Exit.

A study published in the *Journal*: Bascom and Tolle.
"a musician, for example": Naik.
"the laws do not *force*": Supreme Court, Nos. 96-110, 95-1858.
"between letting a patient"; "the withdrawing or withholding":
    Supreme Court, No. 95-1858.
"The only purpose": Mill, page 9.

"Do Not Resuscitate"
    "It is impossible": Swift, quoted by Enright, page 29.
    "there were no differences": Webb, page 176.
    "We use the term *catastrophic reaction*": Mace and Rabins,
        page 41
    I direct my health care provider(s): National Right to Life
        Committee.
    "correct, reverse, or alleviate": National Right to Life Committee.
    "I request and direct that medical treatment": National Right to Life
        Committee.
    "If for moral or religious reasons": National Right to Life
        Committee.
    "My agent shall not authorize": National Right to Life Committee.
    "gives you the chance": Aging with Dignity.

"Chasing Death Down"
    "persistent vegetative state"; patients in a persistent vegetative
        state: "A definition of the persistent vegetative state."
        "Withholding sustenance"; "a medical diagnosis"; "not too
        many years ago": Smith, pages 65–66.
    "Disabled woman"; The news of Cartrette's death; "We're glad we
        intervened": *Sun Journal*, September 1, 2001, page A6.
    Sorrow rusts the soul: Samuel Johnson quoted by Enright,
        page 84.
    "withholding sustenance"; "medical diagnosis"; "Not too many
        years ago": Smith, pages 66, 65, and 65-66 respectively.
    "Just as the strong current": His Holiness the Dalai Lama,
        page 209.
    Now that life: Webb, page 206.

"Is there a moral obligation"; "human beings stricken"; "is not
   abandoning": Paris.
"We all have an obligation": Doerflinger quoted by Webb,
   page 147.
"I have set before you life and death": Deuteronomy 30:19
"If the doctrine of life's essential holiness": Central Council of
   American Rabbis, page 3.
"One is required": Central Council of American Rabbis, page 7.
"There comes a point in time": Central Council of American Rabbis,
   page 9.
"pointless hindrances": Central Council of American Rabbis,
   page 10.
"The removal of an impediment": Central Council of American
   Rabbis, page 13.
"Is it part of the divine plan"; "It underscores"; "the patient's
   'right to die' "; "allowing inevitable death": Sachedina,
   throughout.

"Dementia"
   quem fugis: Virgil, page 16; translation mine.
   Only a small percentage . . . will also burgeon: Conell.
   The Alzheimer's type: Reid.
   How can you tell . . . lying down: The AGS Foundation.

"Hospice"
   Has anyone supposed": Whitman, page 30.
   A study issued in 2002: Last Acts.
   In 1997, only fourteen percent: Webb, pages 63–64.
   despite assertions to the contrary: Lagnado, "Medicare Head
      Tackles Criticism On Hospice Care."
   horror stories; Between 1994 and 1998: Lagnado, "Rules Are
      Rules."
   A report issued in late 2002: Last Acts.
   A study issued in 1997: Webb, pages 236–7.

"The Quality of Life"
   O Rose: Blake, page 85.

"How on earth"; "Is charming and frail Aunt Ella": Gott
"Those who decide": His Holiness the Dalai Lama, page 183.
"chronic dying": Webb, page 53.
"The dilemma we face": Olshansky, Carnes, and Cassel, page 51.
It is not widely understood: Webb, page 128.
"maintaining life": Islamic Center of Blacksburg.
"Compared to traditional care": Last Acts.
Although families bear the impact: Webb, page 209.
The mission of the Project: Project on Death in America.

"Freedom"

At the last, tenderly: Whitman, page 378.

"In the End, Which Is Also a Beginning"

Art lasts, life doesn't: Hippocrates, page 98; translation mine.
"respects the goals"; but recent figures show; "Some of these state policies": Last Acts.

Bibliography

ABCNews.com. Reference: Newsmakers, Jack Kevorkian. [Internet] Available from: http://abcnews.go.com/reference/bios/kevorkian.html.

"A definition of the persistent vegetative state." [Internet] Available from: http://www.geocities.com/HotSprings/Oasis/2919/pvsdef.html.

Aging with Dignity. "Answers to Questions about Five Wishes." [Internet] Available from: http://www/agingwithdignity.org/answers.html.

The AGS Foundation for Health in Aging. "Assessing Pain in Loved Ones with Dementia: A Guide for Family and Caregivers." [Internet] Available from: http://www.americangeriatrics.org/education/dementia.pdf.

Anees, Munawar Ahmad. *Islam and Biological Futures: Ethics, Gender and Technology.* London and New York: Mansell Publishing Limited, 1989.

Barley, Nigel. *Grave Matters: A Lively History of Death Around the World.* New York: Henry Holt and Company, 1995.

Bascom, Paul B., MD, and Susan W. Tolle, MD. "Responding to Requests for Physician-Assisted Suicide: 'These Are Uncharted Waters for Both of Us,'" Journal of the American Medical Association, Vol. 288, No. 1, pages 91–98.

Beam, Jeffery. "The Stroke." Hillsborough, North Carolina: Privately printed pamphlet, 2000.

Becker, Ernest. *The Denial of Death.* New York: Free Press Paperbacks, 1973.

Blake, William. *William Blake,* ed. by Vivian de Sola Pinto. New York: Schocken Books, 1965.

Bridges, Barbara J. *Therapeutic Caregiving: A Practical Guide for Caregivers of Persons with Alzheimer's and Other Dementia Causing Diseases.* Millcreek, Washington: BJB Publishing, 1998.

Britten, Roy J. "Divergence between samples of chimpanzee and human DNA sequences is 5%, counting indels," Proceedings of the National Academy of Sciences in the United States of America, vol. 99, no. 21, October 15, 2002. [Internet] Available from www.pnas.org/cgi/doi/10.1073/pnas.172510699.

Buckingham, Robert W. *Handbook of Hospice Care.* New York: Prometheus Books, 1996.

Byock, Ira. *Dying Well: Peace and Possibilities at the End of Life.* New York: Riverhead Books, 1997.

Byrnes, Glenn. "Dealing with Dementia: Help for Relatives, Friends, and Caregivers." [Internet] Available from: http://www.ncpamd.com/dementia.htm

Central Conference of American Rabbis. "CCAR Responsa: On the Treatment of The Terminally Ill." [Internet] Available from: http://www.ccarnet.org/cgi-bin/respdisp.pl?file=14&year=5754

Cohen, Kenneth B. *Hospice.* Germantown, MD: Aspen Systems Corp., 1979.

Conell, Lawrence J., M. D. "Is It Dementia or . . . ?" Harrisonburg, Virginia: Elder Care Mental Health Group, Rockingham Memorial Hospital, privately circulated handout, 2002.

Daily, Patrick. *Patrick Henry: The Last Years, 1789-1799.* Bedford, Va.: The Descendants Branch—Patrick Henry Memorial Foundation, "The Print Shop," 1986.

Dickinson, Emily. *Poems by Emily Dickinson*, ed. by Martha Dickinson Bianchi and Alfred Leete Hampson. Boston: Little, Brown and Company, 1957.

"Disabled woman caught in guardianship battle dies." *New Bern Sun Journal*, September 1, 2001, page A6.

Enright, D. J., ed. *The Oxford Book of Death*. Oxford and New York: Oxford University Press, 1983.

Exit. "Euthanasia & assisted suicide around the world." [Internet] Available from: http://www.euthanasia.org/else.html.

Gott, Dr. Peter. "The quality of life is the most important issue," *Sun Journal*, New Bern, NC, June 4, 2000.

Hill, Patrick T., and David Shirley. *A Good Death: Taking More Control at the End of Your Life*. Reading, Massachusetts: Addison-Wesley Publishing Company, Inc., 1992

Hippocrates. With an English translation by W. H. S. Jones. Vol. IV. The Loeb Classical Library. Cambridge, Massachusetts: Harvard University Press, 1931.

His Holiness the Dalai Lama. *Advice on Dying: And Living a Better Life*. Trans. by Jeffrey Hopkins. New York: Atria Books, 2002.

Hoffman, Stephanie B., and Constance A. Platt. *Comforting the Confused: Strategies for Managing Dementia*, 2nd ed. New York: Springer Publishing Company, 2000.

Hughes, James J. "Brain Death and Technological Change: Personal Identity, Neural Prostheses and Uploading," Second International Symposium on Brain Death, Havana, Cuba, February 27–March 1, 1995. [Internet] Available from: http://www.changesurfer.com/Hlth/BD/Brain.html.

Humphry, Derek. *Final Exit: The Practicalities of Self-Deliverance and Assisted Suicide for the Dying*. 2nd ed. New York: Dell Publishing, 1996.

Islamic Center of Blacksburg for Islamic Information & Education. "Dying and Death: Islamic View," IQRA'A Newsletter, Vol. 4, No. 3, July 1995.

Jacobsen, Josephine. "The Companions." *The New Yorker*, September 30, 2002, page 137.

Jamison, Stephen. *Final Acts of Love: Families, Friends, and Assisted Dying*. New York: G. P. Putnam's Sons, 1995.

Karnes, Barbara. *Gone from My Sight: The Dying Experience*. Depot Bay, Oregon: privately published, 1986.

Kessler, David. *The Rights of the Dying*. New York: HarperCollins, 1997.

Kübler-Ross, Elisabeth. *Living with Death and Dying*. New York: Macmillan Publishing Company, Inc., 1981.

———.*On Death and Dying*. New York: Macmillan Publishing Company, Inc., 1969.

———.*Questions and Answers on Death and Dying*, New York: Macmillan Publishing Co., Inc., 1974.

Lagnado, Lucette. "Medicare Head Tackles Criticism On Hospice Care, *The Wall Street Journal*, September 15, 2000.

———.Mercy Living," *The Wall Street Journal*, January 10, 1995.

———. "Rules Are Rules," *The Wall Street Journal*, June 5, 2000.

Last Acts. *Means to a Better End: A Report on Dying in America Today*. [Internet] Available from: http://lastacts.org/files/misc/meansfull.pdf.

Lebow, Grace, and Barbara Kane, with Irwin Lebow. *Coping with Your Difficult Older Parent: A Guide for Stressed-Out Children*. New York: HarperCollins, 1999.

Lynch, Thomas. *The Undertaking: Life Studies from the Dismal Trade*. New York: Penguin Books, 1997.

Mace, Nancy L., and Peter V. Rabins. *The 36-Hour Day*. New York: Warner Books, 1999.

Mill, John Stuart. *On Liberty*. Ed. with an introduction by Elizabeth Rapaport. Indianapolis: Hackett Publishing Company, Inc., 1978.

Miller, Lisa. "In Passing: Boomers Begin to Look Beyond the Good Life to the 'Good Death,'" *The Wall Street Journal*, February 25, 2000, Section A, pages 1 and 6.

Moyers, Bill. *On Our Own Terms*. [Internet] Availale from: http://www.pbs.org/wnet/onourownterms/.

Munley, Alice. *The Hospice Alternative: A New Context for Death and Dying*. New York: Basic Books, 1983.

Naik, Gauta. "Last Requests," *The Wall Street Journal*, November 22, 2002, pages 1 and 6.

National Right to Life Committee. "Will to Live Project." [Internet] Available from: http://www.nrlc.org/euthanasia/stateslist.html.

Nuland, Sherwin B. *How We Die: Reflections on Life's Final Chapter.* New York: Random House, Inc., 1993.

Olshansky, S. Jay, Bruce A Carnes, and Christine K. Cassel. "The Aging of the Human Species," *Scientific American,* Vol. 268, No. 4 (April 1993), pp. 46–52.

Paris, John J. "Hugh Finn's 'Right to Die,'" *America,* October 31, 1998. [Internet] Available from: http://www.americapress.org/articles/ParisFinn.htm.

Pipher, Mary. *Another Country: Navigating the Emotional Terrain of Our Elders.* New York: Riverhead Books, 1999.

Project on Death in America. [Internet] Available from: http://www.soros.org/death/index.htm.

Reid, David B. "Is It Dementia?" Harrisonburg, Virginia: Elder Care Mental Health Group, Rockingham Memorial Hospital, privately circulated handout, 2002.

Rollin, Betty. *Last Wish.* New York: Simon & Schuster, 1985.

Sachedina, Abdulaziz. "'Right to Die'?: Muslim Views About End of Life Decisions." [Internet] Available from: http://www.people.virginia.edu/~aas/article/article3/htm.

Sherali, Hanif D. "Medical Law and Science in Islam." Private correspondence, 2002.

Singer, Peter. *Rethinking Life and Death: The Collapse of Our Traditional Ethics.* New York: St. Martin's Griffin. 1994.

Smith, Wesley J. *Culture of Death: The Assault on Medical Ethics in America.* San Francisco, California: Encounter Books, 2000.

Snyder, Lois, and Daniel P. Sulmasy. "Physician-Assisted Suicide," *Annals of Internal Medicine,* 2001; 135: 209–216.

Sun Journal, New Bern, NC, September 1, 2001.

Supreme Court of the United States. Dennis C. VACCO, Attorney General of New York, et al., Petitoners, v. Timothy E. QUILL et al., No 95-1858. June 26, 1997.

———.WASHINGTON, et al., Petitioners v. Harold GLUCKSBERG et al., No. 96-110, 95-1858. June 26, 1997.

Terkel, Studs. *Will The Circle Be Unbroken? Reflections on Death, Rebirth, and Hunger for a Faith.* New York: The New Press, 2001.

Virgil. *The Eclogues and Georgics of Virgil: In the original Latin.* Garden City, New York: Doubleday & Company, Inc., Anchor Books Edition, 1964.

Vorspan, Albert, and David Saperstein. *Jewish Dimensions of Social Justice: Tough Moral Choices of Our Time.* New York: UAHC Press, 1998.

Webb, Marilyn. *The Good Death: The New American Search to Reshape the End of Life.* New York: Bantam Books, 1997.

West, Jessamyn. *The Woman Said Yes: Memoirs.* San Diego: Harcourt Brace Jovanovich Publishers, 1976.

Whitman, Walt. *Leaves of Grass.* Ed. by Emory Holloway. Garden City, N.Y.: Doubleday & Company, Inc., 1926.

Woodman, Sue. *Last Rights: The Struggle over the Right to Die.* Cambridge, Massachusetts: Perseus Publishing, 2001.

Wright, Sam. *Koviashuvik: Making a Home in the Brooks Range.* San Francisco: Sierra Club Books, 1988.

Index